DREAM

Dreams a [most] neglected aspects of our consciousness. Rarely remembered or taken seriously, dreams seem to be only a bizarre series of amusing or disturbing images that our minds create for no particular purpose.

But nothing could be further from the truth! Dreams, through a language of their own, actually contain valuable information about ourselves, which, if properly analyzed and understood, can change our lives. In this fascinating book, the author gives you information that will allow you to begin interpreting—even creating—your own dreams.

You will learn how to understand *dream language* —the symbols that the mind uses to disguise our innermost conflicts. Learn also how to recall dreams, how to keep a dream journal, and how to prepare for sleep so that you will dream more effectively. Look in the extensive *Dream Dictionary* for the meanings of hundreds of dream images.

But most importantly, this book will tell you how to practice *creative dreaming*—consciously controlling dreams as you sleep.

By understanding dreams you will not only understand yourself better but will also understand others and their relationship to you. *Dreams and What They Mean* will provide anyone with the knowledge necessary to begin practicing dream analysis, which Freud called the "royal road" to the unconscious mind. Once a person learns to control their dreams, their horizons will expand and their chances of success will increase a hundredfold!

About the Author

Migene González-Wippler was born in Puerto Rico and has degrees in psychology and anthropology from the University of Puerto Rico and from Columbia University. She has worked as a science editor for the Interscience Division of John Wiley, the American Institute of Physics and the American Museum of Natural History in New York, and as an English editor for the United Nations in Vienna, where she lived for many years. She is the noted author of many books on religion and mysticism, including the widely acclaimed *Santeria: African Magic in Latin America, The Santeria Experience,* and *A Kabbalah for the Modern World,* and *The Complete Book of Spells, Ceremonies & Magic.*

To Write to the Author

We cannot guarantee that every letter written to the author can be answered, but all will be forwarded. Both the author and the publisher appreciate hearing from readers, learning of your enjoyment and benefit from this book. Llewellyn also publishes a bi-monthly news magazine, and some readers' questions and comments to the author may be answered through this magazine's columns if permission to do so is included in the original letter. The author sometimes participates in seminars and workshops, and dates and places are announced in *The Llewellyn New Times.* To write to the author, or to ask a question, write to:

Migene González-Wippler
c/o THE LLEWELLYN NEW TIMES
P.O. Box 64383-288, St. Paul, MN 55164-0383, U.S.A.
Please enclose a self-addressed, stamped envelope for reply, or $1.00 to cover costs.

ABOUT LLEWELLYN'S NEW AGE SERIES

The "New Age"—it's a phrase we use, but what does it mean? Does it mean that we are entering the Aquarian Age? Does it mean that a new Messiah is going to correct all that is wrong and make the Earth into a Garden? Probably not—but the idea of a *major change* is there, combined with awareness that the Earth *can* be a Garden; that war, crime, poverty, disease, etc., are not necessary "evils."

Optimists, dreamers, scientists. . . nearly all of us believe in a "better tomorrow," and that somehow we can do things now that will make for a better future life for ourselves and for coming generations.

In one sense, we all know there's nothing new under the Heavens, and in another sense that every day makes a new world. The difference is in our consciousness. And this is what the New Age is all about: it's a major change in consciousness found within each of us as we learn to bring forth and manifest powers that Humanity has always potentially had.

You still have to learn the "rules" for developing and applying these powers, but it is more like a "relearning" than a *new* learning, because with the New Age it is as if the basis for these had become genetic.

Other Books by Migene González-Wippler

A Kabbalah for the Modern World
Santeria: African Magic in Latin America
The Santeria Experience
The Complete Book of Spells, Ceremonies, & Magic
Rituals and Spells of Santeria
The Seashells
Tales of the Orishas
The Complete Book of Amulets and Talismans

Llewellyn's New Age Series

DREAMS
AND WHAT THEY MEAN TO YOU

Migene González-Wippler

1992
Llewellyn Worldwide, Ltd.
St. Paul, Minnesota, 55164-0383, U.S.A.

FIRST EDITION
Fourth Printing, 1992

International Standard Book Number: 0–87542–288–8
Library of Congress Catalog Number: 88–48183

Cover Art: Victoria Poyser Lisi

Library of Congress-in-Publication Data:
  González-Wippler, Migene.
    Dreams and what they mean to you / by Migene
González-Wippler.
      p.   cm. — (Llewellyn's new age series)
      Reprint. Originally published: Merit Publications,
1980.
    ISBN 0–87542–288–8
    1. Dreams. I. Title. II. Series.
    BF1091.G66   1989   88–45183
    135'.–dc19   CIP

Llewellyn Publications
A Division of Llewellyn Worldwide, Ltd.
P.O. Box 64383, St. Paul, MN 55164-0383

Table of Contents

Introduction

Dreams!

We spend, on average, one-third of our life sleeping, and a portion of that in dreaming.

For the Ancients, dreaming was a method used to obtain knowledge and healing, and it was employed deliberately and scientifically under the guidance of trained therapists and priests.

Yet, we in the modern world have very little knowledge and even less understanding of the nature of dreams or of the levels of consciousness accessed by them.

We know next to nothing about the deliberate use of DREAM POWER.

We *all* dream. That's a scientific fact. Some people rarely remember their dreams or even that they have had dreams. Laboratory research, however, not only proves that we all dream but also that people deprived of their dreams (by being awakened as "REM" sleep starts) rapidly become both psychologically and physically ill. Not only is sleep vital to our health, so is dreaming!

Why?

Because dreams are part of our total consciousness. Our dream life is as vital, although different, as our waking consciousness.

Once that realization is accepted, then the next step is to realize that our casual attitude towards dreaming is a mistake—a mistake as dangerous as lack of nutritional awareness in our daily diet, careless personal hygiene, and stupidity behind the automobile wheel.

We make a mistake in thinking that dreams are merely amusing or frightening interludes between our days of waking consciousness. In most cases, our benign neglect of them does no more than deprive us of the opportunities for a richer and more complete life that can be ours when we pay them due attention. In other cases, such neglect not only deprives us of specific knowledge and guidance to resolve severe and even life-threatening problems, but also can—in some rare circumstances—bring the risk of aberrant, compulsive behavior and the failure to distinguish between dream and awake life.

The truth is that our awake life represents only a very small portion of our total consciousness— less than ten percent. Our dream life represents only another small portion of the total consciousness, but is itself a "doorway" into still greater dimensions: worlds wherein there are psychic and spiritual resources of greater powers, in their own way, than even nuclear power in the ordinary world.

How do we access these other worlds and dimensions? First, by paying attention to our dreams, and then by learning to understand their messages, *and then by learning to communicate our needs and goals from the awake life to the dream life.* Yes, you can learn to control, and enter into, your dream life!

This remarkable book shows you how easily this is done, and what great benefits will be yours in doing so. There is no area of your life that will not respond favorably to the techniques given here. DREAM POWER can bring you success and money in the mundane world, lead to romance and pleasure, improve your marriage and sexual enjoyment with your spouse, provide direct answers to important questions and guidance to better health, and open inner doors to spiritual growth and attainment.

The method is easy. And very rewarding.

But it cannot be done without deliberate effort on your part. Everything you need to know is presented in these pages, and exact step-by-step guidance—along with a complete and practical dream dictionary, one of the vital tools to understanding your dreams—is laid out for you.

Don't waste that one-third of your life that can give you access to the other 90 percent of your consciousness! Start now, start tonight! Suddenly you will start really living 24 hours a day, and those hours will be enriched with as much as ten times greater consciousness. You take control of your life as you take control of your dreams.

DREAM POWER is yours.

Carl Llewellyn Weschcke
Publisher

Chapter 1

Understanding the Human Mind

I believe it to be true that dreams are
the true interpretation of our inclinations;
but there is art required to sort and understand them.
—Montaigne, Essays II, xii

Since his early beginnings man has been fascinated by the mysteries of his own mind. He has tried to penetrate the intricate labyrinths of his mental processes in myriad ways. But still, even today, in spite of the many discoveries and advances in the field of psychology, man still asks himself the eternal question: *What is Mind?*

Plato's Definition of Mind

Many great intellects have endeavored to answer this question. Plato defined mind as a God-given spiritual quality that was totally separated from what he called the "gross material body." Our physical senses—sight, touch and hearing—often deceive us. But through reason, rooted in mind, we may arrive at true knowledge and understanding. To Plato, reason was a vehicle by means of which our sensorial experiences and memories of past experiences could be used as materials for a process of synthesis, analysis and classification that would help us to understand the world around us. Ideas, a term coined by Plato, were certain qualities or essences of mind which we learned to identify as "permanent realities," and which constantly imparted their unchanging form and character to our transient lives on earth. Among such ideas, he cited beauty, truth, faith, hope, and all abstract thoughts.

Aristotle's Argument

Plato's famous disciple, Aristotle, had somewhat different views than his great master. To Aristotle, the body had mysterious psychic powers, which he associated with the existence of the soul in man. By soul he meant the vital energy that is present in all living things. In its most primitive aspect, the **nutritive** soul, it keeps all live bodies feeding, growing and reproducing their kind. As the **sensitive** soul, it feels emotions and sensations and is the seat of memory. Finally, as the **reasonable** soul, it thinks, judges and reasons. It is mind. Therefore, Aristotle, unlike Plato, believed that both the senses and the mind had a common link in the human soul. But both Plato and Aristotle agreed on one basic thing: the awesome powers of the mind.

After the death of Aristotle, nearly two thousand years elapsed before another great philosopher decided to find new answers to the question of mind. This was Rene Descartes, undoubtedly the greatest of French philosophers.

Descartes' Discussion

Descartes, best known for his famous statement, "I think, therefore I am," redefined thinking as the whole range of conscious mental processes, including feelings, sensations, intellectual thoughts and will. He deepened the division that Plato had made between mind and body by insisting that sensation was a function of the mind rather than of the body. In fact, Descartes believed that all of man's animating processes were controlled by the mind. His most daring theory was that the mind had "innate" ideas it was born with. He also believed that the mind is always at work, even during sleep.

Descartes' theories created a veritable beehive of controversy among the scholars of the time. Some, like John Locke, totally rejected them. Others, like Baruch Spinoza, accepted them, albeit guardedly.

Of all Descartes' contemporaries, Spinoza was perhaps the most important because of the influence he was to have centuries later on one of the most innovative thinkers of all times, Sigmund Freud.

The Birth of Psychology

When Freud was born in Austria in 1856, the science of psychology was in its infancy. It had been born barely six years before, on October 22, 1850, when a German professor named Gustav Theodor Fechner decided that the mind and its relation to matter could be scientifically measured. Ten years later, Fechner wrote his famous work, *Elements of Psychophysics*, where he gave the world his technique on how to measure mental processes.

Fechner's studies were followed by those of Wilhelm Wundt, whose prime interest was in sensation. Wundt conducted numerous experiments during which he attempted to break down experience into elements of sensation. During these experiments, students in his laboratory stared at flashing lights, listened to metronomes and pricked each other with needles. Their purpose was to analyze what they heard, saw and felt. Wundt's first important work, *Principles of Physiological Psychology*, was pulished in 1874.

The pioneer work of Fechner and Wundt was followed by many scientists on both sides of the Atlantic. In the United States, William James, the illustrious brother of the novelist Henry James, turned his attention to the human consciousness, which he described as both continuous and selective. His great book, *The Principles of Psychology*, which he published in 1890, is still used as a college textbook.

Division Develops

By the middle of the 1910s, two schools of experimental psychology had been developed. One was the American school of Behaviorism. The other was the German Gestalt school. The Behaviorists believed that the study of man's actions can help understand the reasons for his behavior, thereby shedding light on his mental processes. The Gestalt psychologists, on the other hand, dealt with perception. Their main thesis was that we always tend to perceive the whole before we perceive its parts.

This led them to believe that immediate, meaningful perception is arrived at by the mind's ability to create relationships. Thus, we learn a song's tune before we learn the notes and perceive the form and the beauty of a rose before we become aware of its petals, its stem and its leaves.

The Behaviorism and the Gestalt schools are still active at present, and although their approaches to the study of mind are completely different, they often blend their varied points of views.

Freud's Unconscious

While the Behaviorist and the Gestalt psychologists were concerned with the workings of the conscious mind, in Vienna, Freud was deeply involved with the study of *the deep unconscious mind.* After graduating as a doctor in 1885, Freud had gone to Paris for a while to study hypnosis under the supervision of the famed teacher and neurologist Jean-Marie Charcot. Freud's interest in Charcot's methods was primarily directed at the Frenchman's use of hypnosis in the treatment of hysteria.

When Freud returned to Vienna, he began in earnest the development of his theories about the unconscious. After a short and abortive attempt at work in collaboration with Josef Breuer, a fellow physician, he set out to work alone on his belief that emotions and unconscious motivations were the prime movers of our lives, rather than intelligence. These ideas, as well as his belief in the importance of infantile sexuality in the development of the personality, alienated a great number of his colleagues, who believed that man was essentially a rational being. For a while, Freud found himself ostracized from the rest of the scientific community, but his faith in his theories never wavered, and eventually the world had to recognize the importance of his contributions to the field of psychology.

Freud's Repression

Freud believed that the average individual rejects all hostile and destructive impulses, as well as socially unacceptable forms of sexual gratification. These antisocial urges are very distasteful to acknowledge by the conscious self of a civilized human being. Awareness of these urges arouses anxiety in the individual, who blocks the negative impulses by means of a process which Freud called "repression."

Freud's Sex Drive

The theory of repression was followed by Freud's theory on human sexuality. He called the sexual instinct "libido," and pointed out that the sexual life of an individual begins at the moment of birth. In his view, a person's libido could be satisfied in many ways, such as strenuous physical activity, sports and creative outlets. The libido is often repressed because of the demands of society upon an individual. This creates great conflict within the personality. Thus, other outlets have to be found to ease the anxiety the repressed sexual instinct causes to the individual.

Freud believed that the sexual instinct was one of two major drives in the personality. The second drive was the self-preservation instinct. These two drives he combined into one urge, the "life instinct," which he called "Eros." He believed that the life instinct was able to divert another basic drive, the "death instinct," away from the individual concerned and direct it instead towards others in the form of outward "aggression."

The Id, Ego and Superego

Further observation of human personality, especially in battle-shocked soldiers, led Freud to suggest the personality division which was to form the backbone of Freudian psychology. In this division, Freud saw the human personality formed of three closely interrelated parts: the **Id,** the **Ego** and the **Superego.**

The **Id** is totally unconscious, and is composed of primitive urges and instincts that seek gratification without regard to the consequences to the individual.

The **Ego** is the conscious part of the personality and stands between the Id and the real world and acts as a mediator between the two.

The **Superego** is partly conscious, and urges the individual to resist the negative impulses of the Id and practice instead the highest and most noble of human ideals. It acts in a sense as a "conscience," and judges severely between good and bad behavior. Obedience to the impulses of the Superego promotes feelings of happiness and well-being, while disobedience makes the individual feel guilty and worthless.

The Ego's Function

The Ego, caught between the conflicting demands of the Id and the Superego, undergoes severe tensions and conflict. The result of this struggle and how it affects the Ego is what forms the human personality. When the Ego is successful in harmonizing the urges of the Id and the Superego, the result is a healthy, well-balanced personality. When the Ego fails in harmonizing them, the personality can be damaged and a neurosis or acute anxiety will follow. If the damage is so extreme that the Ego can no longer function, psychosis or mental illness is the result.

The repressed impulses of both the Id and the Superego continually strive for expression and gratification, thus exerting a strong, powerful influence on the personality. The individual cannot describe these impulses but they surface in disguised symbolic imagery in slips of the tongue, lapses of memory and in dreams.

Dreams as Clues to the Unconscious

Freud was quick to realize that dreams could give him invaluable clues to the repressed feelings that caused a psychological disorder in a patient. He eventually evolved a theory that explained that dreams are the best possible record of the human unconscious. The reason why dreams are always symbolic in essence, according to Freud, is that very often they represent an unconscious wish that is socially unacceptable or too frightening or unpleasant to be allowed into outer consciousness, even in the form of a dream. Therefore, they are disguised in symbolic form. In this way, they can be released from the unconscious, relieving it of anxiety and repression, without offending the sensibilities of the outward, conscious personality.

Free Association

In the beginning of his psychological practice, Freud used the techniques of hypnosis he learned from Charcot, but soon he realized this system had too many inadequacies that hindered his progress. Some of his patients could not be hypnotized at all. Those who could be did not always respond to his suggestions. This led Freud to search for an alternative approach to the unconscious, until he eventually developed a technique he called "free association." His patients were asked to lie down on a couch in Freud's study and talk about the first thing that came to their minds. Freud discovered he could trace strong emotional drives and the sources of mental anxieties and neuroses in the often disconnected ramblings of his patients. This was to be the birth of psychoanalysis.

Dreams, however, remained the main source of information on the hidden workings of the human unconscious. In 1900, Freud published his classic work on the subject, *The Interpretation of Dreams*, which is still in use today by modern psychology.

Jung Joins the Search

Of all Freud's followers, the most famous was Swiss psychiatrist Carl Gustav Jung. Concepts like *extroverted* and *introverted* are some of Jung's lasting contributions to the field of psychology.

Although fascinated by Freud's ideas of the unconscious, Jung soon parted company with Freud because of the latter's great emphasis on sexuality. Jung's doctrines, which were to be known eventually as Analytical Psychology, were deeply influenced by myths, mysticism, metaphysics and the religious experience. Freud's work was too materialistic and biological in its orientation and did not agree in principle with Jung's belief in the importance of the historical and spiritual side of man. When Jung published his revolutionary work *Psychology of the Unconscious* in 1912, the formal break between the two great men was completed.

Jung Differs

Jung redefined some of the Freudian terms in the development of his psychology. Ego, for instance, he redefined as the complex of representations which constitutes the center of an individual's consciousness and which appears to possess a very high degree of continuity and identity. Jung saw the Ego as an "autonomous complex," which was at the center of the consciousness. Thus we see that whereas to Freud the Ego formed all the components of the conscious personality, to Jung the Ego is only the focus of personal identity, the **Me,** while the consciousness is the manifestation of the individual's awareness of himself and of the outer world.

Another Freudian term redefined by Jung was *libido.* To Freud, this word meant the entire complex of human sexual impulses. To Jung, it signified the energy of the processes of life. Jung often used two terms interchangeably to describe the energy that operates in the psyche. One of the terms was libido and the other was **psychic energy.** The main difference between Freud and Jung's concept of libido is that Jung works with a larger and more flexible concept of energy. To him, libido or psychic energy has two aspects. One is cosmic energy, the other is energy manifested specifically in the psyche of man.

Consciousness as Defined by Jung

Jung also broke away from Freudian psychology in his concept of the various levels of consciousness. He conceived the psyche as having three layers. At the surface is Consciousness; below it is the Personal Unconscious; and at the base is the Objective or Collective Unconscious.

Consciousness contains the attitudes of the individual, his Ego, his approaches to external environment. It is also the seat of his rational and logical processes. It is not only the face he presents to the world, but also his awareness of that world and how he copes with it.

The Personal Unconscious houses the psychic contents that have been repressed from consciousness either deliberately or unknowingly, as well as those urges that have not yet reached the coscious aspect of the personality. In many ways, the Personal Unconscious resembles Freud's concept of the Id, but Jung conceived of it only as the "more or less superficial layer of the unconscious." It contains fantasies, dreams, and ideologies of a personal character, which are the result of personal experiences, things forgotten or repressed.

The Objective or Collective Unconscious is the largest and deepest area of the psyche. Jung believed this part of the human unconscious is the seat of the memories of all humanity, and contains the roots of the four psychological functions: sensation, intuition, thought and feeling.

The Collective Unconscious is the container of all latent memory traces of man's entire history. It is common to all human beings and harbors within all the knowledge and wisdom of the past. Thus, in principle, according to Jung, *the human unconscious has all the answers to every possible question about man's beginnings.* All our latent fears, desires and inclinations also come from the Collective Unconscious, and both the Ego and the Personal Unconscious are built upon it.

Archetypes

A large part of the Collective Unconscious consists of those basic components of the human psyche Jung called the **archetypes.** An archetype is a universal concept containing a large element of emotion and myth.

The concept of the archetype is very important in the understanding of dream symbology because it explains why some dream images seem to have a universal meaning that applies to all members of the human race, while other images are highly personalized and only concern each individual dreamer.

Jung conceived the archetype as an "autonomous complex," that is, a part of the psyche that detaches itself from consciousness to such an extent that it appears to be independent from the rest of the personality and to lead an autonomous life of its own. This in itself is not an abnormal condition, provided it is only allowed to highlight certain aspects of the personality and that the consciousness maintains full control over all the various parts of the psyche.

The main types of autonomous complexes or archetypes conceived by Jung as parts of the psyche are the Persona, the Shadow, the Anima and the Animus, and the Self. These archetypes appear in dreams in the form of figures that may or may not be known to the dreamer.

The Persona

The Persona is the mask that the individual wears in his daily life, the face he presents to the outside world. It is, in other words, his conscious personality. The Persona is identified with the Ego, and it appears in dreams in the form of a figure that embodies those qualities that typify the Ego. If the individual is severe in his/her general outlook on life, the Persona may appear in his/her dreams as a stern old man. On the other hand, if the individual is "devil may care" in his/her attitude, the Persona may be represented by a clown or a child.

Because the Persona represents the individual's

conscious attitude, it is placed in the psyche as an opposite of the unconscious. This means the contents of the Persona are in a constantly tense relationship with the unconscious. Any extremes that the individual builds in his persona will be counteracted by opposite extremes in the unconscious. For example, if a person presents to the world an overly moral and conservative face, he will suffer great torments from completely opposite unconscious urges. Thus, it is very vital for mental health to endeavor to build a reasonably well-balanced Persona that is harmonious to the individual and not difficult for him/her to maintain.

The Shadow

The Ego tends to develop the strong side of its personality and to integrate it into its conscious attitudes and thus into the Persona. The weaker aspects of the psyche are then gathered, unwanted, into the unconscious, and there they form another autonomous complex or archetype known as the Shadow. This is the dark side of the personality, and it surfaces from time to time to embarass and generally to harass the individual. It appears in the conscious personality without warning, as sudden moods and urges that lead the individual to do and say things that are generally contrary to his usual behavior. This sometimes happens when the tension between the Persona and the unconscious is so great that large amounts of libido or psychic energy are released by the psyche. This libido left undirected and unchannelled turns back into the unconscious and causes old repressed urges and desires to overflow into the conscious aspects of the psyche. This overflow is the archetype known as the Shadow.

The Shadow Knows

Very often, normal instincts and creative impulses are relegated to the realm of the Shadow along with the negative and destructive side of the Ego. For that reason, it is vital for each individual to accept this darker aspect of his/her personality and try to understand and channel this psychic energy along constructive paths so that it will not overpower his consciousness, threatening his/her normalcy and well-being.

The interplay between the Ego and the Shadow is not unlike the struggle between Dr. Jekyll and Mr. Hyde in the Robert Louis Stevenson novel. Thus, we can say that the Shadow is the worst side of an individual, the part of him/herself he either refuses or fails to accept and recognize.

In dreams, the Shadow may appear as a vague, often threatening figure, difficult to discern with clarity. It is invariably antagonistic and usually frightening. Other times it shows up under the guise of an enemy or someone equally detested by the dreamer.

One of the best ways a person can identify some of the contents of his Shadow is by observing his most negative reactions about things and his intense dislike of certain qualities or faults in other people. Those things he abhors so much are the very same things that occupy the core of his Shadow. He must therefore understand this truth about himself because in so doing he will become a better balanced individual.

Anima and Animus

The Anima and the Animus are the concentration of those characteristics of the opposite sex that exist in every human being. The Anima is the hidden female in every man. The Animus, likewise, is the hidden male in every woman.

In a man, the Anima is the center of the emotional, instinctive and intuitive side of the his personality. This archetype is formed of a conglomeration of all the women a man has known in his life, especially his mother. The integration of the Anima will enable a man to develop his sensitive, spontaneous, receptive nature, and allow him to become less aggressive and instead become warmer and more generous and understanding. On the other hand, the repression of his female characteristics will result in obstinacy, hardness, rigidity, and sometimes in irresponsibility and drunkenness.

The Animus in a female acts in a very similar way as the Anima in the male. The ability of a woman to take well-calculated risks, make split-second decisions, be strong, level-headed, independent and self-assured, all of these qualities are male characteristics embodied in her Animus. When a woman ignores this aspect of her nature, she becomes whining, fretful and insecure.

When an individual comes to terms with the

Animus or Anima, he or she will have a better understanding of the opposite sex, and will be able to extend the full range and potential of his or her personality.

In dreams, the Anima appears to a man in the figure of a woman with no face, or an unknown face. In a woman's dream, the Animus appears as a group of men or a man with contrasting qualities. Because the Anima and Animus are the result of a transformation of the Shadow, the appearance of either of these two archetypes in dreams may be accompanied by the intrusion of disagreeable unconscious impulses into the conscious personality.

But there is a positive side to this situation. While there will be a period in the individual's life marked by disturbances in normal behavior patterns, the emergence of the Anima or Animus indicates that the integration of the personality is now under way. This personality integration was called the "Individuation Process" by Jung.

The Individuation Process

When the Individuation Process is completed, a new and most important archetype emerges from the psyche. This archetype is the Self. At this point, the Anima or Animus, which is the symbol of the unconscious and of all the archetypes, loses its force, releasing great amounts of psychic energy or libido into the psyche. This libido comes to rest in a "twilight zone" where it acts as a bridge between the conscious and unconscious aspects of the psyche. The harmony that is created when the conflict of opposites expressed by the conscious and the unconscious is resolved is the embodiment of the Self. The Ego or Persona finds itself revolving around the Self, which is now the center of the psyche and the source of all its energy.

The Higher Self

The Self as an archetype symbolizes the higher spiritual aspect of man. It is the Atman, the Higher Self, the Holy Guardian Angel, the Buddha Self, the god within. It is the highest ideal to which man can aspire.

When the Self appears in a dream it usually indicates that the Individuation Process is being completed, and that the personality is being integrated successfully. In a man's dream, the Self in its totality appears as the Wise Old Man. In a woman's dream, the figure appears as the Great Mother. But in each case, the Self has four main aspects that represent the four qualities of the psyche. These four aspects have both a positive and a negative side, as shown in Table 1.

The negative aspects of the ideal Self archetype are the remnants of the integrated contents of the Shadow. Whenever they appear in a dream they indicate that their particular forces are being ignored by the individual and that they must be recognized and accepted before full individuation can take place. The Self becomes an integrated whole when all the different aspects are individually developed and absorbed into the personality.

Table 1

The Great Mother	The Wise Old Man
Intellect	*Intellect*
Amazon (positive)	Hero (positive)
Huntress (negative)	Villain (negative)
Intuition	*Intuition*
Priestess (positive)	Joker (positive)
Evil Witch (negative)	Black Magician (negative)
Emotion	*Emotion*
Princess (positive)	Youth (positive)
Seductress (negative)	Tramp (negative)
Sensation	*Sensation*
Mother (positive)	Father (positive)
Terrible Mother (negative)	Ogre (negative)

As stated earlier, *the archetypes are part of the Collective Unconscious, and as such they have universal meanings. When one of these archetypes appears in a dream it has similar connotations for all human beings. The personal parts of a dream are not archetypal in essence, although they can represent aspects of the dreamer's unconscious.*

Importance of Jung's Theories

The reason why we have dwelt so extensively in the various psychological schools, and Jung's theories in particular, is that in order to understand the symbology of dreams, and even why we dream at all, we must have a working knowledge of the structure of the human mind or psyche.

Jung's theory of the Collective Unconscious and the archetypes, although often criticized and disparaged, still remains one of the most viable and lucid explanations of the mysteries of the mind. His concept of the libido, the Individuation Process, and his dream theories are all very helpful in the interpretation of dreams, and ultimately in the integration of the personality.

But even Jung himself balked at the thought of a stereotyped, rigid theory of dream interpretation. He stubbornly reiterated that there was "no general theory of dreams." Likewise, there are no fixed meanings for the symbols of the unconscious. It always depends on the dream and specifically on the dreamer. This belief is strongly shared by this author. Therefore, in this guide, although dream interpretation will be conducted along psychological lines, great emphasis will be placed on each individual dreamer and his immediate environment.

Chapter 2

Why Do We Sleep?

Death, so called, is a thing which
makes men weep,
And yet a third of life is passed
in sleep.
—Lord Byron, Don Juan, XIV, iii

Every night we go to sleep and, with some rare exceptions, become "dead to the world" for a period of time that extends on the average to approximately eight hours. Some people spend considerably less time sleeping, while others spend more.

Newborn babies, for example, sleep an average of 17-18 hours a day. Adolescents sleep approximately 10-11 hours in a 24-hour period, while young adults spend an average of eight hours a night sleeping. Elderly people, on the other hand, seldom sleep more than six hours during the night. This seems to indicate that we require less sleep as we grow older, but still, on the whole, we spend approximately one-third of our lives sleeping.

Circadian Rhythms

An immense amount of research is being conducted all over the world on the phenomenon we call sleep. Some amazing discoveries have been made on this, our secret night life, but the most puzzling question still remains essentially unanswered. Why do we grow increasingly dazed every night, until our bodies become clumsy and inoperative, our eyes close unwillingly, and our minds blank out for several hours? This mysterious lethargy that is sleep affects not only human beings but practically every living thing in nature.

Even plants seem to follow a cycle that includes sleep. Some flowers close their petals at night and open them again in the morning, as if they were aware of the transition between night and day. Scientists call these cycles **circadian rhythms,** which are daily fluctuations comprising a 24-hour period. These cycles are presumed to be present in every living cell.

Thus, the whole of nature is engaged in one huge circadian rhythm. Examples of this phenomenon are ocean tides, the setting and rising of the sun, the four seasons, the mating of animals, a woman's ovulating period, and the gestation of mammals.

Sleep is also believed to be controlled by circadian rhythms; that is, we sleep because an internal "clock" in our brains gives the signal for our bodies to stop their daily activity and go into slumber for a certain amount of time.

This cessation of activity takes place usually at night because our bodies are less functional at this time. Our minds are less receptive to learning, our body temperature lowers, our reflexes are not as quick; in short, we are at a low ebb in our mental and physical mechanisms.

Jet Lag

When we alter our sleeping habits, losing several hours or more of sleep, the body reacts with feelings of fatigue, nervousness or irritability. Scientists believe this is due to a "phase shift" of our circadian rhythm.

Jet lag is a typical example of such a shift. If we fly from California to New York we may have trouble falling asleep the first night because our bodies are still operating on Pacific Time, which is three hours earlier than the Eastern Standard Time which operates in New York. And even if we should sleep a full eight hours, we would still find it difficult to awake at eight o'clock the next morning because our internal clocks would tell our bodies it is only five o'clock.

After several days in New York, our bodies would adapt to the change in the time schedule. Upon returning to the West Coast, we would find ourselves three hours ahead of Pacific Time, and again we would need a few days to adjust to the change. A "phase shift" does not mean, therefore, we have *lost* sleep, but rather that "body time" is out of phase with "clock time."

What Happens When You Don't Sleep?

Actual sleep deprivation, where a person loses more than one night's sleep, does tend to affect the organism, impairing several faculties of the body. After three nights without sleep, the average person complains of itchy eyes and begins to see double. He/she is unable to count past 15, cannot concentrate on any subject for longer than a few minutes, and begins to lose his/her sense of balance. He/she also feels lightheaded and often hears a buzzing sound in his/her ears. In some cases, if the loss of sleep continues, the person begins to develop marked paranoid symptoms.

In 1959, a New York disc jockey named Peter Tripp decided to stay awake for 200 hours in order to raise money for the March of Dimes. During the beginning of the marathon, he was in good spirits and made a daily broadcast from a glass booth in Times Square. But toward the end of the 200 hours, his speech became slurred and incoherent, and soon thereafter his behavior became pronouncedly paranoid.

These psychotic tendencies made their appearance during the nighttime hours, at which time Tripp became convinced that unknown enemies were trying to drug his food in order to force him to fall asleep. This persecution mania was accompanied at times by auditory hallucinations.

Tripp went on to complete his 200-hour sleepless marathon, and soon thereafter recovered from his temporary paranoia. The only treatment he required was a healthy dose of sleep.

Necessity of Sleep

Since Tripp's experience, many researchers have devoted considerable time and effort to studying the effects of lack of sleep in the human body, and specifically, in the human mind. With some rare exceptions, they have discovered that sleep deprivation is detrimental to the perfect internal harmony of man. Even animals show negative effects in the absence of sleep, and baby animals, such as kittens, will die if they are not allowed to sleep for several days.

Those people who allegedly feel no ill effects in the absence of sleep are probably unaware of the existence of short sleep periods known as microsleep. This means that a person may doze off for a few seconds without realizing it. These short sleep periods may then repeat themselves intermittently throughout the night, providing the individual with enough sleep to function normally.

Why We Need Sleep

So we know that pronounced loss of sleep is detrimental to the body and the mind. In other words, we *need* sleep. The question is *why*.

Experiments by NASA have shown that the relief of body fatigue is not the specific function of sleep. We do not sleep only to rest. On the other hand, Navy studies have proven that prolonged isolation decreases the need for sleep in an individual. This would seem to indicate that less interaction with other people and less outside stimuli would result in a need for less sleep.

Sleep control centers are located in the brain stem, which is an area the size of one's little finger at the base of the brain. Scientists believe the brain stem contains a system whose activity ensures wakefulness in the individual, while its inactivity leads to sleep.

Russian Nobel Laureate Ivan Pavlov, who was a neurophysiologist, believed the brain's natural state is wakefulness. In other words, the brain is always awake and active, and its activity is only interrupted for the restoration and recovery of the body.

During sleep, the body is only functioning at a very low level, stressing the important role played by the brain in keeping it awake. This role is dramatically emphasized in sleep disorders such as apnea, where a person cannot breathe while asleep, and narcolepsy, where a person will fall asleep every few minutes, regardless of the time and place he may find himself. People afflicted with these tragic diseases can never hope to lead a completely normal life, at least until science can find both the reason and the cure for these disorders.

If Pavlov's theory is correct, as many scientists seem to believe, and the brain's natural state is wakefulness, and if rest is not the specific function of sleep, why sleep at all, especially considering that the body is functioning at a lesser level during sleep?

Nature is immensely logical and prosaic in its evolutionary processes. It seldom commits blunders, and when it does, they are seldom of major importance. Therefore, the evolution of such a complex organism as man, with a thoroughly wasteful timing device such as unnecessary sleep worked in, seems inconceivable.

The act of falling asleep is the result of lying down and relaxing the body. After some time has elapsed, the heart and respiration rate will decrease, blood pressure will be lowered, and body temperature will drop below its normal level. If the individual continues to lie still without moving, he will eventually fall asleep. But he will never know exactly when because even with the help of an electroencephalogram it is impossible to determine the exact moment a person falls asleep.

What typifies the onset of sleep is the loss of awareness. We fall asleep at the exact moment an external stimulus, such as a noise, fails to evoke a response in us.

REM and NREM

Scientists have discovered that there are two types of sleep. These have been called REM (Rapid Eye Movement) and NREM, pronounced "non-REM."

The NREM state is the first sleep period of the night. It is often called the "quiet sleep" because it is characterized by slow, regular breathing, an absence of body movements, and decreased brain activity. The sleeper has simply lost contact with his/her environment due to his/her brain's lethargy. He/she is no longer receiving information through his/her five senses and, therefore, he/she is not reacting to his/her surroundings. The body is able to move during this stage but it does not because the brain does not tell it to do so.

There are several NREM periods during the night. The first one lasts approximately 80 minutes. It is immediately followed by the first REM period, which usually lasts about ten minutes.

The REM period is characterized by small, convulsive twitches of the hands and facial muscles. If the individual has been snoring, he/she stops, and his/her breathing becomes irregular and labored. His/her body becomes completely paralyzed, and he/she is unable to move his/her arms, legs or trunk. Blood pressure usually soars during this period and the heart beat increases as if the sleeper were running an obstacle course. Most significantly, the eyes begin to move rapidly from side to side under the closed eyelids, as if the sleeper were looking at a moving object.

Researchers have discovered that if a person within the REM stage is awakened he/she will invariably say that he/she has been dreaming. Thus, the REM sleep period has been identified with the dreaming state in the human being, although the same phenomenon has been noticed in animals, leading scientists to think that humans may not be the only ones to dream.

All during the night the NREM and the REM stages of sleep alternate with each other. The cycle varies from 70 to 110 minutes, but the average is 90 minutes.

In the beginning of sleep, the NREM periods are longer, but as the night progresses, REM periods grow longer, at times lasting for as long as one hour. Thus, in general, we can say that we dream approximately every 90 minutes throughout the night, and that we dream roughly two hours out of every eight-hour sleep.

Need for REM Sleep

Advanced sleep research has uncovered the fact that REM sleep is needed by the human being. Individuals who have volunteered to sleep and be observed in sleep laboratories have reacted very negatively when they have not been allowed to complete any of their REM periods. They became nervous, irritable, and erratic in their behavior, and slept badly and uncomfortably.

So, the general conclusion has been that *sleep is necessary, particularly the portion of sleep that is connected with dreaming. Many scientists believe that THE ONLY REASON WHY WE SLEEP IS SO THAT WE MAY DREAM.*

Babies, who sleep between 16 and 18 hours a day, spend more than 50 percent of this time in the REM stage. Does this mean that babies are dreaming all during this time? If so, what about? *Could their unconscious minds be releasing from the Collective Unconscious enough stored information to prepare each baby for his/her new life?*

And what about the rest of us? Why do we dream?

Could it be that we dream so that our unconscious minds may unravel and absorb the problems and happenings of each day, incorporating them into the neat filing system of the Collective Unconscious?

Maybe a dream is the way the unconscious mind copes with things, helping the individual interact satisfactorily with his/her environment. In other words, perhaps at least some dreams bring to bear on the individual dreamer's problems and needs the resources of the Collective Unconscious— the total, cumulative experience of Humanity that we all share in at this level!

For that reason, sleep deprivation, particularly REM sleep, is detrimental to the individual's health and well-being. Significantly, one of the first indications of mental illness is a marked disturbance in the person's sleeping patterns.

But what is a dream? What causes it and how is it produced? Most importantly, what does it mean to us in our waking lives?

Chapter 3

What Is a Dream?

> *All that we see or seem*
> *is but a dream within a dream.*
> —Edgar Allan Poe, A Dream Within A Dream

During Freud's time, dreams were believed to be the "guardians of sleep." One dreamt in order not to wake up. Whenever a disturbance arose in the vicinity of a sleeper, the brain manufactured a dream that would prevent the individual from being awakened.

Freud himself felt that dreams were interwoven around the noise or outside stimulus to form a story that would safeguard the person's sleep.

For many years this theory persisted, even after the discovery of REM sleep. A dripping faucet, the sound of a siren or an alarm clock, the need to urinate, or a full stomach were all considered the prime suspects in the causation of dreams, and even in the onset of REM sleep itself.

But eventually this theory was disproven because it has been shown in laboratory experiments that the REM period, and thus dreaming, is determined by a biochemical process which is circadian (cyclic) in nature, and *not* caused by outside influences.

*A dream can incorporate a disturbing stimulus into its plot, but it cannot be **initiated** by this stimulus. In other words, dreams are not instantaneous occurrences, but very well-planned ones.*

The Stuff Dreams Are Made Of

The dream experience can vary widely between individual dreamers. To some, the actions in a dream follow logical sequences, while to others, dreams are irrational and illogical.

Some people have symbolic, abstract dreams, while others have realistic dreams as normal as waking life.

Some dreams can seem intensely real, while others are so fantastic that we become aware that we must be dreaming.

Dreams can be alternately dull and exciting, creative and destructive, frightening and enjoyable.

Some fulfill our wishes, others frustrate them.

A dream can depress us to the point of tears or fill us with hope and inspiration. Sometimes they seem to control us, and sometimes we control them.

Some people can dream at will, and some can return to a dream they started the night before.

But whatever the "stuff dreams are made of," the important thing is they seem to be real to the brain.

Jung believed that the unconscious mind is the

"matrix" of dreams, and that therefore dreams were the exponents of the human psyche. He also believed that dreams provide the bulk ot the material necessary for the proper investigation of the psyche, and that dream interpretation on a large scale would, after some time, surrender the complete programming of an individual's mind.

Contrary to Freud, Jung believed that outside organic sensations did not cause a dream. This view was to be confirmed many years later in sleep laboratories, as we have seen. Instead, Jung felt that dreams are the remnants of a "peculiar psychic activity" taking place during sleep.

Freud's Dream Theories

Nevertheless, Freud's theories on dreams laid the groundwork for much of the research that was to be conducted on the subject by other workers, including Jung. Some of Freud's ideas have been disproved, but others remain at the core of modern dream theories.

Central to Freud's theory of dreams was his wish-fulfillment theory. According to Freud, dreams are essentially the result of repressed wishes that come to the surface of our consciousness when we are asleep. These wishes, unacceptable to the conscious personality, are satisfied and fulfilled during dreams, but in symbolic form only. So well-disguised are these repressed desires that we are unable for the most part to identify them when we awake.

The mental agency responsible for the distortion of dream images was named first the Censor by Freud, and then the Superego. The idea behind the distorted dream is to keep the sleeper from waking up, by expressing the repressed wish in veiled terms.

Freud believed that the mind works in two totally opposite ways. The first type, which he called the Primary Process, is characterized by symbolization, ignorance of the concepts of time and space, and wish-fulfilling hallucinations.

The second type, known as the Secondary Process, is governed by reason and logic, observance of time and space, and learned adaptive behavior.

The Primary Process is exemplified by the state of dreaming and the Secondary Process by conscious thinking.

Freud believed the dream state or Primary Process preceded the conscious state or Secondary Process, and that the latter, as well as all ego development and the acquisition of a thinking apparatus, depends largely on the repression of the dreams and hallucinations which are part of the Primary Process. In other words, we dream before we think. This theory was Freud's major contribution to the understanding of dreams.

Also according to Freud, a dream has two sets of "contents." One of these sets, the *latent* content, is the true message of the dream, what the unconscious is trying to say to the conscious personality.

The second set is known as the *manifest* content and it represents the actual dream remembered by the dreamer. In other words, the latent content of the dream is translated into the symbolic imagery which is known as the manifest content. Again, the purpose of these masquerades is to prevent the sleeper from waking up.

Freud's Dream Analysis Method

The best way, according to Freud, that one can decipher the convoluted symbolism of dreams, is by discovering the first idea that occurs to the dreamer when he thinks of his dream, and then following it to see where it leads, or where it meets with a mental block.

The idea behind this theory is that all the associations with the various details of the dream will eventually disclose a recurrent theme, which will be the message of the unconscious, or the latent content of the dream. This system of dream elucidation was called by Freud **free association.**

Jung also used free association in his dream interpretations, but he did not share Freud's belief that *all* dreams are the result of wish-fulfillment. He felt some wish-fulfillment is present in some dreams, but not in all.

Jung's Dream Theories

To Jung, our lives are spent in the midst of struggles in order to realize our wishes. If we cannot fulfill these wishes in reality, then we do it in a fantasy, in a dream. The use of free association comes in when we try to discover the experience or experiences that caused this dream or fantasy. Jung called this use of free association, **amplification.**

Some people feel that it seems useless to have dreams if we cannot understand them. But this, strangely enough, is not true. We can reap benefits from a dream whether we understand it or not. This is because the unconscious uses a different type of language than that of the conscious mind, and it also offers a totally different point of view. This amounts to a psychological adjustment, a "compensation" which is absolutely necessary for a proper balance between conscious and unconscious actions.

When we are awake, we reflect on every problem with the utmost care. But often we go to sleep with our unsolved problems very much present in our minds. The unconscious mind continues our exploration of the problem on a deeper level. It is able to grasp aspects of our problems we either ignored or were unaware of. Through dream symbology the unconscious helps us to cope with our problems, even in those instances when the problems cannot be immediately solved.

We awaken from the dream with a sense of balance, with the feeling that we can and will overcome our problems. That is the reason some people like to "sleep" on a problem, while everyone feels "like new" after a good night's rest. We simply dream our cares away.

Listening to Our Dreams

While it is true that we do not have to understand our dreams to benefit from them, it is also true we can enhance their effect considerably if we try to understand them. This is often necessary because "the voice of the unconscious" is easily ignored and seldom heard.

In order for us to understand the voice of the unconscious, we have to become familiar with the language it speaks. This language, as we have seen, is largely symbolical. The symbolism of dreams can be interpreted through either a *causal* or a *final* standpoint.

Dream Symbolism

The causal standpoint, which was used by Freud, starts from a desire or craving—that is, from a repressed dream-wish. This craving is always something comparatively simple, which can hide iteself in a great variety of ways.

For instance, a repressed sexual impulse can be expressed in a dream as putting a key in a lock to open a door, flying through the air, or dancing.

To the typical Freudian, all oblong objects in a dream are phallic symbols, while round or hollow objects are feminine symbols.

In other words, the causal standpoint gives a fixed meaning to each symbol in a dream, regardless of who is the dreamer.

Specific Individual Symbolism

The final standpoint gives each image a specific meaning. These meanings vary, not only between individual dreamers but also between different dreams. In this system, dreaming of opening a door means an entirely different thing than dreaming of flying through the air.

Which of these two standpoints do we use in

interpreting a dream? According to Jung, we should use both.

> *The causal standpoint provides the fixed meaning that has been given to a specific symbol by the collective unconscious. This means that every symbol has a fixed meaning for every human being.*
>
> *The final standpoint gives a second meaning to the same symbol, namely that which the dreamer associates with that particular image. This is the personalized aspect of a dream, and that which makes it individual.*

Jung held the interesting idea that the abstract and figurative language of dreams, which is reminiscent of the Biblical use of parables and of the symbolism of primitive languages, could well be the survival of an archaic mode of thought used by man in prehistoric times.

Dreams are often in opposition to our conscious plans. This is not always very marked. Sometimes it is a subtle deviation from the conscious attitude, but occasionally it coincides with the conscious plans. This behavior of the dream is called **compensation** by Jung, and it means a balancing and compounding of different data and points of views in order to produce adjustment and rectification between the conscious and the unconscious aspects of the personality.

Dream Interpretation

Although the conscious attitude of a person may be known, the attitude of the unconscious is not. This can be learned through dream interpretation.

When the conscious and the unconscious are unbalanced, this can be very dangerous for the individual, as the unconscious is very capable of destroying the personality if left to its own devices. The correct interpretation and understanding of dreams can help reveal any dangerous rifts between the conscious and the unconscious, in time to effect the proper harmony between the two.

Jung identified several types of dreams. The **compensatory** dream, which has just been described, adds to the conscious mind all those elements from the previous day which remained ignored either because of repression or because they were too weak to reach consciousness. In a sense, this dream acts as a self-regulation of the psyche.

Dreams of Prediction

The **prospective** dream is an anticipation of future conscious achievements or happenings, a form of advance blueprint of the individual's life. Its symbolic contents may outline the upcoming solution of a conflict or prepare the dreamer for a distressing future occurrence.

Although the prospective dream is often called prophetic, Jung tells us that in the vast majority of cases they are merely an anticipatory combination of probabilities that may coincide with the actual development of things.

This is not surprising because a dream is the result of the fusion of repressed elements and is therefore a combination of all the feelings, thoughts and ideas that have not been registered by the consciousness. In other words, *dreams know things we do not and are, therefore, in a better position than we are to predict the outcome of many things.*

Telepathic Dreams

Although he felt that the majority of prophetic dreams were prospective and naturally explainable, Jung also believed that there are some dreams that are decidedly telepathic and that no amount of learned dissertation can change that truth. Some people seem to have this ability and often have telepathically influenced dreams.

Jung did not attempt to offer a theory for this phenomenon, but he believed that most telepathic dreams are affected by a powerful human emotion, such as love or grief. Thus, most telepathic dreams predict the arrival or the death of a loved one, or any happening that will deeply affect the dreamer.

Nightmares

The **nightmare**, which haunts so many of man's dreams, is a compensatory dream of vital significance for the consciousness because it often warns the individual his conscious actions are threatening his/her well-being.

We invariably have nightmares if we overeat or otherwise overindulge our senses. We also have "bad dreams" when we are doing something reprehensible or socially unacceptable. It is our unconscious way of saying we are endangering our physical or mental balance. If we persist in our negative actions, the nightmares may get worse, and the unconscious will find a way of either correcting our behavior or destroying our personality and us.

Other Disturbing Dreams

Reductive, or negative, dreams are dreams that bring the dreamer down a notch or two. The people who have these dreams have an unusually high opinion of themselves and are constantly impressing it on others. The unconscious mind, who knows perfectly well there is a lot of hot air in these balloons, perversely sets out to burst them in a colorful explosion of horrid imagery.

Jung used to recall with great gusto the dreams of one of his patients, a pedantic aristocrat who held herself in great esteem, but who would go to sleep at night only to dream of dirty fishwives and drunken prostitutes.

Reaction dreams reproduce experiences we have had. These are often caused by traumatic experiences and will repeat themselves until the traumatic stimulus is exhausted. When the reaction dream is recognized through dream interpretation, it usually stops from reoccurring.

Recurrent dreams are particularly present in youth, although they can also make their appearance in later years. The recurrent dream can be very disturbing because it invariably leaves us with the impression that they must have a special meaning. We feel haunted by the recurrent dream.

This feeling, according to Jung, is invariably correct because this type of dream is usually caused by a psychic disturbance. The identification of the latent content of this dream usually marks the end of its occurrence.

The Uncommon Dream

Most dreams, however, can be more simply divided into two groups, namely, the "little" dreams and the "big" dreams. The little dreams are very common, and are mostly of the compensatory type. They are easy to identify because they are equally easy to forget.

The big dreams, on the other hand, are never forgotten. They often contain symbolic images of an archetypal or mythological nature. Godlike figures, princes, castles, dragons, snakes, lightning bolts, the Wise Old Man, Christ are typical of this type of dream. These figures come from the collective unconscious and usually have an important message for the dreamer.

These dreams occur in critical phases of life, and we have all had at least one of these dreams. It is the kind of dream that makes us say, "I will not forget that dream as long as I live." And we usually don't.

Common Symbols

There are some symbols that reoccur in everyone's dreams. Typical among these are dreams of flying, of climbing stairs or mountains, of falling, of hotels, of trains, of weddings and of being naked.

These symbols are known as **dream motifs** and give some support to the theory that there is a fixed meaning to dream symbols. These motifs become particularly significant in a series of dreams of a recurrent nature.

Dream Interpretation

But how about the method to interpret these great variety of dreams? Jung did not offer a simple system for dream interpretation, but he had several important suggestions.

1. One of these is to make sure that every shade of meaning which each detail of the dream has for the dreamer is determined by the associations of the dreamer him/herself. This means that every individual who wishes to decipher his/her own dreams should attempt to find meanings to each detail of his/her dreams by writing down the first thing that comes to his/her mind in connection with that particular motif. This should be followed through with as long a list of associations as possible for each symbol. This should reveal to the individual what personal meaning each symbols has for him/her. This procedure was called by Jung "taking up the context."

2. The causal, or fixed, meaning of each symbol should also be taken into consideration, and a dictionary of dreams can be useful for this purpose, as it gives the accepted traditional meanings of dreams.

3. Lastly, and perhaps the most interesting of Jung's suggestions, is that one should turn to the past and reconstruct former experiences from

the occurrence of certain symbols in his dreams. This should tell us what type of happening we can expect after dreaming with a certain motif.

If we combine these three methods, we should be able to interpret our dreams with relative ease. In the process, we would be learning much about our unconscious attitudes and would be creating a greater harmony between the conscious and the unconscious aspects of our personalities.

Chapter 4

The Symbology of Dreams

*For 'tis not doubtable, but that
the mind is working, in the dullest
depth of sleep.*
—Owen Felltham, Of Dreams, c. 1620

We already said that there are two sets of meanings to every dream, the **latent** and the **manifest.** The **latent** meaning is the true message that the unconscious is trying to convey to the conscious personality. As this message emerges from the depths of the unconscious mind, it becomes translated into symbolic imagery which is then presented to the consciousness in dream form. This imagery comprises the **manifest** meaning of the dream.

Why Do We Dream in Symbols?

Why does the unconscious use symbols to convey messages to the conscious personality? Freud believed the reason for this need of disguising the true message was to prevent the sleeper from waking up. This explanation does not satisfy many psychologists and dream experts, who believe that the reason we dream in symbols is that symbology is the language of the unconscious.

In other words, we think and even feel in symbols. The reason for this phenomenon is that we are constantly bombarded by visual images during our waking periods. Many of these images are registered by our eyes and by our unconscious minds, but not by our conscious awareness.

Again, many of these images, even the ones we consciously acknowledge, are not accompanied by either sounds or explanations for their existence. They are simply recorded and stored in our mental depths and quickly forgotten by our conscious minds. Many of these images resurface during our dreams in connection with any specific problem or thought we had at the same time we saw that particular thing. To our unconscious mind that visual image became a symbol of the problem or thought we were entertaining at the time. It is interesting to note in this context that blind people have dreams that are totally lacking in visual imagery.

From the preceding it is easy to understand why most psychologists have concluded that many of the symbols that appear in dreams are directly related to visual images which have been seen by the dreamer at one time or another, most often during the previous day. This would tend to make the interpretation of dreams rather difficult without a knowledge of the circumstances surrounding each individual dreamer.

However, there is still another set of symbols that reoccur in everyone's dreams, regardless of the images we see during the day. These are the symbols Jung called dream **motifs**, and which tend to support the theory that there is a fixed meaning to some of the symbology that is part of the deep unconscious.

As we said earlier, some of the most typical dream motifs are dreams of falling, of flying, of climbing stairs or mountains and of riding in trains, buses or automobiles. Dreams with death or with the dead, as well as dreams of weddings, of teeth, of ships, or nakedness and swimming or drowning are also common.

We all have dreamt about all or almost all of these motifs, and in practically all cases the meanings seem to be the same. Of course, we must always analyze each dream in the context of each dreamer's private life. But dream motifs as such seem to share the same meaning in all members of civilized societies. This would tend to place these particular symbols within the realm of the collective unconscious, which, as we have seen, is the common working ground for all human minds. Dream motifs are the subject of all dream dictionaries, including the one presented here.

Colors and Numbers in Dreams

Strangely enough, although our waking life is vibrant with rich colors, not all our dreams have colors in them. It is true that some people seem to dream in color all the time, but they are in a small minority, because it has been ascertained by several competent researchers that most people have more dreams in black and white than in bright technicolor. Actually, the term "black and white" is misleading because colorless dreams seldom show a distinction between any hues. They are rather drab in tone and the hues seem to belong to the dullest ranges of gray and brown.

Calvin Hall, perhaps the greatest modern authority on dreams, collected thousands of dreams during his research studies, and was able to report eventually that only 29 percent of the recorded dreams had been in color.

As to the most common colors which appear in dreams, Dr. Fred Snyder, a pioneer in dream studies, found that the most recurrent color in dreams was green, with red following close behind. Yellow and blue were only half as common as green.

Dr. Patricia Garfield, another dream researcher, made a special analysis of her own dreams and discovered that color appeared more often in her dreams after several hours of rest. Dr. Garfield concluded that there may be a common chemical base for the occurrence of colors in dreams and that perhaps the cerebral cortex is more aroused when the body has been at rest for some time.

Cayce's Color Theory

Edgar Cayce, the famed "sleeping prophet," believed that sometimes color in a dream is used to underline certain conditions in our lives in order to heighten our awareness. To Cayce, bright, clear colors were indicative of positive aspects or trends in our lives, while muddy, drab colors had negative associations. A combination of green and blue in a peaceful setting could be an indication of healing of mind or body, while deep greys or dark browns could show a pessimistic outlook for any given situation surrounding the dream.

According to Cayce, personal likes and dislikes in colors affect their meaning in dreams. For example, if you prefer green over any other color and you have a dream where green is the most predominant color, this would mean that your unconscious is giving you an optimistic message about the particular situation depicted in the dream. On the other hand, if you loathe the color green, to see it in a dream would indicate you have deep negative feelings about the subject of your dream.

Meanings of Color

In general, colors in dreams have been adjudicated the following meanings:

Black—the color of death, indicating depression and moodiness in the dreamer.

Blue—spiritual energy and high ideals; fidelity; cool intellect; the celestial, and therefore, the high aspirations of the soul; deep blue means intuition and understanding.

Brown—the color of the earth, therefore it means sensation and sometimes disintegration.

Gold—the color of the sun, therefore it means the conscious mind and truth; it also indicates the masculine principle.

Green—vitality, healing; growth; hope; the principle of life itself; a muddy green indicates jealousy or weakness and inexperience.

Orange—health; energy; occult powers; the power of mind; messages.

Pink—the emotions; love; joy; illusion.

Purple or violet—vital power; the moon color and therefore intuition; maybe travels or news.

Red—life force; sexual passion; blood; fire; also anger.

White or silver—purity; peace; light; illumination; wisdom; a symbol of the moon, and therefore of the female principle.

Yellow—sunshine; mind; intuition; pure energy; happiness to come; good financial prospects; a muddy yellow indicates cowardice and sometimes death.

Naturally, the type of object we see surrounded by a specific color in a dream is just as important as its hue, and we have to take both meanings into consideration before reaching a reasonably accurate interpretation of the dream.

Number Symbology

Numbers are also important in dream interpretation, and they have been the subject of extensive research on the part of psychologists.

To Jung, for example, numbers predated man and in fact had been discovered rather than invented by human kind. Jung went one step further and stated that "it would not be such an audacious conclusion after all if we define number psychologically as the archetype of order which has become conscious." This means that the unconscious uses numbers as "ordering factors," that is, as a means of creating order in the universe. In other words, *each number has a specific meaning for the unconscious mind, a meaning that is the same for each individual member of the human race.*

Some ancient languages were structured upon the same belief. The Hebrew language, for example, still in use, uses the same characters for both letters and numbers. Each Hebrew letter and therefore each number, represents a cosmic state and has a specific meaning.

In modern times, each number from 0 to 9 has also been ascribed a special meaning. When the number is larger than 9, its digits are added until the number is reduced to one digit, not larger than 9. This is done because there are only ten pure ciphers, each one indicating a state of mind. These ciphers extend from 0 to 9. When a composite number seems very significant, instead of reducing the number to one digit, it is far more enlightening to look at each of the individual ciphers that compose the number and find each of their meanings. One can then apply these meanings to the problem presented in the dream, and find an inner guidance to its possible solution.

However, there is another instance when the larger composite numbers should not be reduced to a single digit, or even analyzed in terms of the individual ciphers. If such a number appears as significant in a "big" dream, then it will have a symbolical meaning all its own—a meaning that may be revealed in an intuitive flash, through meditation, or through an understanding of **gematria.**

Gematria, part of the ancient Hebrew Kabbalah, recognizes certain numbers as having *archetypal* meanings that can be explored through established "correspondences," or associations of words having similar numerical values. One valuable reference to this system is *Godwin's Cabalistic Encyclopedia*, pubished by Llewellyn Publications. Another is *777* by Aleister Crowley, published by Samuel Weiser.

Meaning of Numbers

Following is a list of the most accepted meanings ascribed to numbers.

One—the ego, the individual; an unconscious cry for independence and originality; a need for self-expression; an indication to speculate, act, create, move ahead on your own; a symbol of the sun.

Two—indicates indecision, worry over the possibility of a forthcoming change; stresses the need for calmness and diplomacy; warns against abrupt changes and impulsive actions; a symbol of the moon and therefore of intuition.

Three—this is a symbol of expansion and humor; a promise of good fortune to come; but it also warns against confusion and doing too much all at once; new happy contacts to be made; the symbol of the Trinity, therefore it often indicates family unions; the number of Jupiter.

Four—the symbol of the square and therefore an indication of trials to come, which can only be overcome through hard work and self-control; four is also a symbol of fate and solidarity; anything connected with four will stay for a long time in a person's life, perhaps bringing great changes in its wake. This number is associated with Uranus and with the four elements.

Five—strong indications of sexual activity and romance; also of change, travel and variety; a symbol of communication and freedom; it encourages the individual to search for new ways of contact with others, to move; the number of Mercury, the planet associated with communications and messages; also represents the five fingers of the hand and is a symbol of life.

Six—indicates changes in the home or immediate environment; shows a need to investigate family and financial conditions before making any serious move or decision; also an indication to be generous, forgiving and sympathetic with erring loved ones; the number of Venus, a planet associated with love, generosity and diplomacy.

Seven—a warning against self-deception; you may be looking at a person or a situation in an illusory manner; indicates a tendency to loneliness, pride and independence; a warning against signing any important papers; a need to be careful and analytical of people and situations; a number of the planet Neptune, and thus of illusion.

Eight—an indication of added pressures and responsibility, but with material gain in the end if the individual is willing to work hard; a powerful number that is connected both with sex and with death or transformation; business investments are favored if the person is willing to accept increased activity; this number promises money in large quantities, but again, only if the individual is willing to work hard; the number of Saturn, and therefore a symbol of great activity, power and ambition.

Nine—known as a perfect number, nine is a symbol of completion, of perfection and spiritual attainment; this number indicates a need to move on one's own, to avoid hangers on, to make any necessary breaks with old ways in order to succeed; a time to travel and change environments; a need to look toward the future with hope, for it promises great things; the number of Mars and of aggression.

Zero—indicates a gestation period; a time for introspection and waiting; a new cycle approaches; regeneration and sometimes death; zeroes added to a digit, such as 10, 100 and so on, indicate a higher cosmic state or a higher state of awareness connected with the original digit; for example, if number 1 means the ego, 10 would represent the mind and 100, the soul. Higher numbers would represent cosmic states that would be beyond the comprehension of the human intellect.

Gambler's Numbers

There is another set of meanings attributed to dreams and numbers which has come down to us through many diverse traditions. These are the numbers that are popularly used for betting and gambling purposes. In these cases, each dream motif has also been ascribed a special number that may comprise one or more digits. No one knows for sure the origins of this custom, but many professional gamblers scan their dreams carefully in search for clues of winning numbers. In the dream dictionary included with this guide, each dream motif will be accompanied by its ascribed number.

Time and Space

Often in dreams the symbology with which we are faced fails to indicate whether we are observing a past, present or future event. This happens because the human unconscious moves in a space-time continuum where past, present and future exist simultaneously along various points of space. This means that the unconscious mind does not differentiate between time spans, and therefore does not make any efforts to distinguish between the past and the future, the present and the past, or the present and the future.

Nevertheless, because time moves in space, we can ascertain time in dreams if we observe the position of objects in a dream. For instance, approaching objects usually denote the future and receding objects, the past. An immovable object usually represents the present. Some psychologists believe that objects on the right side of the dream "picture" tend to relate to the future and those on the left, to the past. The possible solution to a problem is sometimes indicated by a door, an elevator or a fork on the road.

Do Dreams Foretell the Future?

But can a dream truly foretell the future? The

answer is yes, according to the innumerable case histories recorded by dream researchers.

This phenomenon, which Jung called the **prospective** dream, can be explained through the ability of the unconscious mind to bring to the surface of the consciousness events from the future. In other words, the unconscious mind seems to know what is going to happen, and this knowledge extends infinitely in time. The knowledge of future events can be made known to us through dreams, as well as through telepathy, clairvoyance or clairaudience.

Jung explained this extraordinary power of the unconscious mind as the principle of **synchronicity.** According to Jung, many circumstances in a person's life that are dismissed as "coincidences," are in reality *meaningful* in the sense that they are messages from the unconscious mind.

Examples of this type of coincidence are the telephone call or the letter from a person about whom we were just thinking; the "hunch" that turned out to be correct; the dream that foretold an event that took place a few days later. Not coincidences, said Jung, but examples of synchronicity, or the harmonious working of all human minds within the conglomerate which is the collective unconscious.

Sex In Dreams

Sex is sometimes explicit and other times implicit in our dreams. This means that some of our dreams are openly concerned with sex, and others use symbols to denote sexual activity.

Notable among sexual symbols in dreams are very physical activities such as dancing, flying through the air or riding a horse. Always take special note of the individual with whom you dance in a dream, for that person is assuredly a very desirable sexual playmate to you either consciously or unconsciously.

It is important also to note that person's attitude toward you in the dream, for that is also a message from your unconscious to you. If the person seems uninterested or unwilling to dance with you, chances are you are wasting your time entertaining any amorous thoughts towards him or her. On the other hand, if your dancing partner seems eager and pleased to be in your company, you can be sure that person will be very receptive to any sexual advances on your part.

Open sexuality in dreams usually denotes sexual repression in the dreamer's daily life. These dreams are often "wish fulfillments," and should be treated as such. Sometimes people become very concerned with dreams of abnormal sexual activity, such as homosexual encounters, bestiality or plain exhibitionism.

Most psychologists advise against taking this type of dream seriously, as it may often express an aspect of the dreamer's own self. Making love to a person of one's own sex could be simply an expression of self-love, a message from the unconscious that we should take better care of the self. A dream with an animal could be a reflection of our lower instincts, and exhibitionism could indicate a need to be more open to others.

The sexual dream should be interpreted in the same manner as any other type of dream—the unconscious' message duly noted and heeded, and then the dream dismissed. It is unwise to worry over this or any other type of dream, for any excessive concern about any given subject tends to affect the delicate balance of the human mind.

The Dream's Purpose

What the dream and its symbology is doing is helping us to "digest" the problems and occurrences of our daily lives. By means of dreams, the unconscious helps us to adapt to each day's changes and the challenges we are continuously facing. When a dream is threatening, the unconscious is telling us that there is a situation around us, depicted in the dream, which is out of control, and which we should try to overcome. Invariably within that same dream's symbology, we can find the solution to that particular problem.

Our personal problems, our fears, our likes and dislikes, our hopes, and our needs, all of these are reflected in symbolic form in our dreams. That is why we must take into consideration all the circumstances that surround us when we interpret a dream.

The purpose of dream interpretation is to try to understand the language of the unconscious mind and to listen to its suggestions and explanations. This is of vital importance because when we understand the message from the unconscious mind, we also understand what makes us "tick," and are in a better position to control and direct our lives.

Chapter 5

The Nightmare

Her lips were red, her looks were free,
Her locks were yellow as gold:
Her skin was white as leprosy,
The Nightmare Life-in-Death was she,
Who thicks man's blood with cold.
—Coleridge, The Ancient Mariner, III

We are all familiar with the nightmare. We have all experienced the pounding heart, the sweating body, the labored breathing, the feeling of horror and impending disaster which are associated with this nighttime terror. But what causes the nightmare? Why does the human unconscious release a poisonous stream of terrifying images at certain given times during our sleep?

Overeating and the Nightmare

Some scientists advise against going to sleep immediately after a large meal because they believe a full stomach can be the culprit in a great deal of nightmares. We all know Dagwood of the famed *Blondie* cartoons and his weakness for monster-

sized sandwiches. The consumption of these strat-
ospheric concoctions was invariably followed by a
monster-sized nightmare, well-seasoned with a few
monsters of its own. In keeping with the old adage,
we can say that many a truth is said in jest, and this is
also the case in Dagwood Bumstead's nightmares.

The reason why overeating can lead to nightmares is twofold. First of all, there is usually a feeling of guilt connected with overeating. This guilt is
reflected in the punitive actions of the terrifying
characters of the nightmare. They chase, threaten,
attack, and generally bully the dreamer into a state
of nervous collapse. These self-inflicted terrors seem
almost designed to deter the dreamer from overeating again before going to sleep.

The second aspect of this situation to be considered is the fact that the monsters and threatening
figures in the nightmare are images released by an
overactive brain working double time to process
digestion and keep watch over the body as the
individual rests. A great many chemical substances
are at work in the body at this time, and the increased
activity of both brain and heart, which should naturally be working less during sleep, tends to bring
out the most negative images stored in the unconscious. It is almost as if the unconscious mind were
getting even with the conscious aspect of the personality for making it work at a time when it should
be able to relax.

Drug Abuse and the Nightmare

But overeating is not the only cause of the

nightmare. Drug abuse, as well as sudden drug withdrawal, can also result in the most nerve-shattering nightmares.

Dr. William C. Dement, a world-famous authority on sleep and dream phenomena, has determined that sleeping pills can cause what he calls "profoundly disturbed sleep." Dr. Dement says that many people who start taking sleeping pills to alleviate their insomnia find after some time that they need increasingly large doses of the medication for it to be effective. Eventually, their dependence on the sleeping pills is so great that they can no longer sleep without them. Whenever they attempt to sleep without medication, they either cannot sleep at all or else they sleep only to be tormented by terrifying nightmares.

Dr. Anthony Kale, who does sleep research at the Pennsylvania State University Medical School, has confirmed Dr. Dement's findings on the sleep disturbances connected with drug abuse and drug withdrawal.

Recurrent or continuous nightmares are so disruptive of the normal thought patterns of the mind that they are considered by psychiatrists to be one of the first symptoms of an impending nervous breakdown. This does not mean that every bad dream should be seen as the precursor of mental collapse, but recurrent or persistent nightmares, accompanied by other sleep disturbances, should be promptly consulted with the family physician or with a competent psychologist or psychiatrist.

Other Causes

But what causes the recurrent nightmare or any nightmare that is not sparked by overeating or drugs?

Dr. Dement thinks that the intensity of brain stem activity and the activation of "primitive" emotional circuits may be what determines the sense of dread in dreams. These primitive circuits are naturally buried in the depths of the unconscious mind and are, therefore, not only difficult to control, but also largely responsible for the release of the most horrible images within the unconscious.

Fear is one of the most primitive urges in the human being, and the things we fear the most, we try to avoid by burying them deep within the unconscious mind. Any sympathetic emotion, such as fear itself, worry, anxiety or insecurity over any given situation, can trigger the hidden mechanisms that activate what Dr. Dement calls the "primitive emotional circuits," causing the flow of the negative imagery we call the nightmare.

Death Symbols in Dreams

Jung, on the other hand, noted that actual death is often announced by symbols that indicate changes, rebirth or journeys. Long trips by train, ship or airplane are particularly suspicious, but only if they repeat themselves constantly over a period of a year.

The same holds true for dreams of moving from one place to another, coming out of deep water, or drowning in it. This latter dream can also indicate the danger of mental illness, as deep water usually symbolizes the unconscious mind.

But again, these findings are not conclusive because these same dreams can simply mean not death but a new growth and transformation of the personality, as it occurs when the individuation process is completed.

What to Do About the Nightmare

What all of this means is that we cannot offer a perfectly valid or clear explanation of the causes of the nightmare. All we know for sure is what to avoid in order not to have bad dreams. We know, for instance, that we should not indulge in rich or heavy meals immediately before going to sleep. We also know that excessive drug use, including the mildest sleeping pill, as well as prolonged or excessive worry, can trigger the nightmare mechanism.

And psychologists also tell us to watch our thoughts immediately preceding the onset of sleep, for they are the most likely ones to surface during our dreams. Disagreeable or frightening subjects, morbid books and films, should all be carefully avoided shortly before going to sleep.

But what do you do if, after carefully avoiding all the suspected causes of the nightmare, you still find yourself battling Dracula and the Wolfman without the benefit of either a Crucifix or a silver bullet? The answer is simple. You must fight back. If Dracula bites you, bite him back. If the Wolfman is chasing you, turn around and give *him* a run for his money. Be as mean and nasty to your monsters as they are to you, meaner and nastier if possible. If you do, you will soon see that your nightmares are not darkening your sleeping time as often as they used to in the past.

But wait, you say, how do I do these things, how do I control my nightmares? Easy. You tell yourself before going to sleep you do not wish to have any bad dreams, but that if they come, you will be prepared to fight them off.

What Do Nightmares Mean?

The reason why it is important for you to fight the nightmare is that *the frightening symbols that occur in a bad dream are in reality all the problems that you fear and the negative qualities within yourself you still have to overcome.* Whenever you face a threatening figure in a nightmare and vanquish it, you have successfully integrated a negative part of you or taken the first step to overcome a problem. You can be sure that specific figure will never threaten you or attack you again in a dream.

I would like to digress at this point and relate a nightmare I had recently which illustrates the preceding point. I dreamt with the archetype Jung called the Shadow, and which is the conglomeration of all the negative traits in the individual. When the Shadow is not fully integrated into the personality, it can destroy you. Unfortunately, its integration takes time and in some cases it is never accomplished.

In my dream, I saw the shadow of a woman moving stealthily about with a long knife, also in shadow, in her extended hand. I knew it was only a matter of time before it turned the knife on me. Almost immediately, I saw my hunch was right. The disembodied shadow turned around and lunged at me with raised knife. "It's you I want to kill," it hissed venomously at me. I was worried because I knew it could hurt me, but I held my ground. "Why do you want to kill me?" I asked it. "Because I hate you," it answered, and moved closer. I still did not budge. And suddenly I was no longer frightened. I felt in total control of the situation in spite of the shadow's threat. "No, you don't hate me," I said. "You love me. You love me very much, don't you?" The shadow lowered its head and the knife fell from its open hand. "Yes, I do," it said sadly. "I love you very much. I just wish I were more like you, but I know that can never be." It then drifted away and that was the end of the dream.

What happened during this dream was that I came face to face with all the negative aspects of my personality, accepted them, and most important of all, was able to control them, forcing them to realize they are still a part of me and therefore should not hurt me. The shadow's sadness because it cannot be more like me is its acceptance that all of its traits must remain hidden because they are socially unacceptable. They can never be expressed consciously, hence, they "can never be." I was inexpressibly relieved with this dream because it marked a new growth in my personality and the integration of my shadow.

The Senoi and the Nightmare

The confrontation of threatening figures during nightmares is the life-long work of the Senoi tribe of the Malay Peninsula. This primitive people have been described by anthropologists as the most democratic group in man's history. They have had no violent crimes or personal conflicts for hundreds of years and are always happy and in perfect mental health.

The Senoi's secret for peace is simple. They use dream interpretation and manipulation for their mental health. The Senoi believe that dream images are part of the individual and are formed of psychic forces that take external forms, like my dream of the shadow.

For this reason, they learn from childhood to master these internal forces. Senoi children are encouraged not only to confront, but actually to attack hostile figures or "spirits" in their dreams. They are taught to call "friendly spirits" to their aid during nightmares. These friendly forces, which can be equated with angelic and religious figures, are the positive inner aspects of the personality. The Senoi believe that any threatening figures destroyed by the dreamer will emerge later on as a friendly spirit or ally.

It is also important, according to the Senoi, not to be afraid of falling dreams. Confronted with such a dream, the individual should let himself fall, whereupon he will discover that the frightening falling dream turns into a pleasant flying experience, with its usually erotic undertones.

Prolonged study of the dream beliefs of the Senoi has led many modern psychologists to conclude that their dream philosophy is the healthiest and most adequate for the preservation of mental health and the integration of the personality.

What has emerged from our brief study of the nightmare is that it is an expression of fears, anxieties and negative traits which we must try at all costs to control. This we can do simply by confronting the nightmare; instead of fearing it, we must attack it and ultimately vanquish it. By doing this we can succeed, not only in solving our problems but also in controlling all that is negative within us.

Chapter 6

Can You Control Your Dreams?

> *Those who dream by day are cognizant*
> *of many things which escape those who dream by night.*
> —Edgar Allan Poe, Eleonora

We said in the previous chapter that ingesting a heavy meal before bedtime can be the cause of terrifying nightmares. Likewise, sounds that penetrate the subtle veil of sleep and are registered by the mind can influence our dreams in a variety of interesting ways. A dripping faucet can be incorporated into a dream as approaching or threatening footsteps, a doorbell can conjure images of weddings, messages or fires, running water can be transformed into waterfalls, floods or dreams of drowning.

In the same manner, the position of the body during sleep can influence a dream with startling results. A person may have dreams of being suffocated, dismembered or being engaged in any number of sexual activities simply by the pressure of bedclothes on his body.

Dreams of nakedness are also sparked by the

weight of bedclothes or by being uncovered in a drafty bedroom.

All these dreams are known as representative dreams, and are often caused by a specific type of automatic excitement of the brain region created by outside stimuli.

Very often, at the first onset of sleep, when a person is beginning to fall asleep, he or she may see a series of strange faces parading quickly before his/her eyes. Sometimes other senses become involved as well, and the dreamer may seem to hear strange voices whispering in his/her ears or calling out his/her name. The feeling of being swallowed by rushing waters is not uncommon during these experiences.

Because of the eerie nature of these images and noises, many people adjudicate mystical or supernatural meanings to these dreams. But again, they are the result of an overly active brain releasing a stream of unrelated images to the surface of the conscious mind. Faces and voices are most common because they are the simplest of all stored mental images and sounds.

Sleepwalking

The phenomenon of sleepwalking or somnambulism has bafffled scientists for centuries. Together with bed-wetting and "night terrors," sleepwalking occurs almost exclusively in small children and those in the pre-puberty stage. Although there have been some instances recorded of adults suffering from these disorders, these cases are quite rare.

Although most doctors agree that there is no definite clue as to the reason for sleepwalking, it has been suggested that these episodes may represent the expression of emotional conflicts that are repressed by the child during waking hours and allowed to be exteriorized during sleep. They can also be caused by hyperactivity in a child; in other words, a child that is always too active for his age and body build may often be the victim of sleepwalking.

Even today, doctor's advice on sleepwalking is not to treat it in any way, as the child will outgrow it before adolescence. Because most treatments are ineffective anyway, they only serve to make the child anxious unnecessarily.

What to do if you are an adult and you find yourself sleepwalking? Here the case is totally different. Sleepwalking in an adult is an indication of a severe anxiety that should be treated by a competent psychologist.

Induced Dreams

The induced dream is *a dream that is planted in the unconscious.* In other words, it is a way by means of which we can learn something about ourselves and our problems and how to solve them.

In the beginning, dreams were used as a means of preventing or curing diseases. Like Aristotle, who believed he could identify an illness by the type of dream dreamt by a person, most of the ancients believed that they could not only identify illnesses through dreams, but also cure them. Notable among the practitioners of dream medicine were Hippocrates and Galen, the fathers of modern medicine.

Inducing dreams in these early times was known as incubation. It consisted in going to a sacred place in order to receive a useful dream from a god. Although healing was one of the most important uses of the induced dream, the incubation was used for a variety of purposes.

For example, in the famous *Epic of Gilgamesh*, the hero appeals to a mountain for a dream shortly before attacking a monster. Gilgamesh and his companions use a magic ritual to achieve this purpose. They hollow out the ground facing the setting sun and from this hole emerges a mysterious sleep, maybe a drug-like vapor, which promptly overcomes the hero. The opening of the earth in this symbolic tale symbolizes the unfolding of the unconscious processes to the conscious mind.

The Yogis also practice dream incubation in what they call the **intermediate** state of dreaming. Three conditions are necessary for the Yogi to evoke the dream desired.

First, during sleep the Yogi must never be unconscious, that is, he must be intensely aware that he is sleeping, and he must be able to control not only his dreams but the objects and people perceived in them.

Second, he must hold himself in a half sleep, the link between sleeping and waking.

And third, before going to sleep, he must do a series of breathing exercises that will place him at the required "junction" between exhaled and inhaled breaths, at the very point were he enters into contact with pure energy. It is this energy that will produce the desired vision during sleep.

In Iran, the dervishes induce dreams by means of a drug mixed with wine. Muslims in general believe that the practice of incubation is part of a holy rite known as the **istiqara**. The dreams that result from this rite are believed to be divine revelations.

Two of the steps taken to induce this type of dream are first of all, to invoke the aid and protection of the individual's eternal "Master" and eternal "Guide," and then to keep the mind from wandering, while at the same time concentrating all thoughts on the desired dream.

Creative Dreaming

There are many cases in both literature and music where the idea for either a literary or a musical masterpiece was found in a dream. For example, both *Treasure Island* and *Dr. Jekyll and Mr. Hyde* were inspired by dreams of Robert Louis Stevenson. Dante's *Divine Comedy*, Du Maurier's *Trilby* and Coleridge's *Kubla Khan* were all examples of masterpieces which were the result of dream inspiration.

Many other famous writers, such as Henry James, Baudelaire, Emily Bronte, Dostoyevsky, Wordsworth and Walter de la Mare, all used their dreams to write unforgettable literature.

Mental Suggestion Through Dreams

Many modern psychologists are convinced that dreams cannot only be controlled by the dreamer, but also that his or her entire life may be altered by means of dreams. These psychologists believe that we can implant positive suggestions in our unconscious minds before going to sleep in order to get answers to our problems from the unconscious in the form of dreams.

Dr. Patricia Garfield, a noted researcher in dream control, says that a dreamer who becomes totally aware of his/her dream state and can hold on to his/her awareness becomes capable of experiencing his/her heart's deepest desires in his/her dreams. He/she can "consciously" choose to make love with the partner of his/her choice; he/she can travel in his/her dreams to distant lands; he/she can speak with any figure he/she wishes, real or fictional, dead or alive; he/she can find solutions to his/her waking problems; he/she can discover artistic creations.

The dreamer who can become "conscious" in his/her dream state opens for him/herself an exciting personal adventure.

But perhaps most important of all, the creative dreamer's greatest advantage over the ordinary dreamer is his/her opportunity to unify and integrate his/her personality. The fearlessness of dream images that the creative dreamer learns to develop produces a mood of capability that carries over into waking life, providing a foundation for confident, capable action. Also, dream control will result in the ability to sustain dream images for long periods of time, as well as in an increasingly stronger capacity for dream recall.

How Do We Learn to Control Our Dreams?

Dr. Garfield has not one, but half a dozen systems that a person can follow in order to make his/her dreams do as he/she wills. The simplest of these methods is the celebrated incubation system of the ancients. In the use of this method, the individual must begin by finding a particularly pleasant and harmonious place for his/her dream experiments, a place where he/she will not be distracted from the subject of his/her desired dream.

The next step to be followed is to clearly formulate the intended dream. It is important also to choose a specific dream topic, and to put one's intention into a concise, positive phrase, such as "Tonight I learn how to solve this or that specific problem," taking care to specify clearly which problems one wishes to solve. One can also decide to have a dream about a special person or about how an illness may be cured.

The important thing to remember is that faith in the dream ritual and determination to succeed are the basic ingredients for the dream's success. One must be determined to receive an answer through a dream and keep concentration firmly anchored on the chosen dream topic.

The next thing to do after the preceding steps have been taken care of is to deeply relax the body through the rhythmic and periodic inhaling and exhaling of air. When the body is in a drowsy, relaxed state, one must repeat the chosen dream topic over and over, concentrating all thoughts on it. At this point, one visualizes the dream as though it were about to happen, and tries to picture oneself after the dream has taken place. In other words, one must believe strongly that the unconscious mind can provide the desired dream.

Dr. Garfield also counsels her students to record all their dreams in the present tense and to do so immediately upon awakening. She also believes it is important to produce positive dream images in some form in waking life. Specifically, she advises to engage in activities related to the desired dream just before going to sleep. This will ensure that the unconscious will receive a clear visual image connected with the dream before sleep, making it easier to achieve the desired dream goal.

Some people have the uncanny ability to wake up in the middle of the night, interrupting a pleasurable dream, and then go back into the dream and continue it where they left off. This type of dream control can also be acquired with perseverance and determination. But perhaps the most desirable aspect of dream control would be to become aware that we are dreaming in the middle of a dream. This is known as the lucid dream and is a common practice among Yogis.

There are several known steps to achieve the lucid dream. First of all, you must accept that all dreams are thoughtforms. This means that every horrible nightmare and shocking dream you ever had was only an expression of your own unconscious mind. Knowing this will make it easier for you to confront a monster in a nightmare and will not leave you so dismayed if you find yourself in an amorous dalliance with a particularly disturbing partner.

The next step in achieving the lucid dream is to determine to remain conscious during your dreams. It is very helpful if you concentrate on the idea of dream consciousness for two or three days before attempting to become aware during a dream. As you become conscious during a dream, you can induce any change you want in it. This will render you fearless of any dream image, no matter how terrifying, because you will have the ability to change that image at will. As you become unafraid of negative symbolism in dreams, you will be able to use your dreams for creative and healing purposes.

Above all, you must remember that, as in all things, achieving control in dreams requires persistence and the determination to succeed. As in the old adage, remember, if at first you don't succeed, try, try again. Eventually you will.

Chapter 7

How to Interpret Your Dreams

> *There's a long, long night of waiting*
> *Until all my dreams come true,*
> *Till the day when I'll be going*
> *Down that long, long trail with you.*
> —Stoddard King, "There's a Long, Long Trail"

As we have seen, some of our dreams do come true. And this happens because the human unconscious moves on a space-time continuum where past, present and future blend into infinity. The prophetic or prospective dream is part of the phenomenon Jung called synchronicity, which we discussed in Chapter 5. There is no doubt that the prophetic dream does take place. What is curious is the fact that not all of our dreams come true and that we are seldom able to foretell ahead of time which of our dreams are prophetic and which are not.

The Prophetic Dream

What all prophetic dreams have in common is a quality of forewarning. Nothing of real importance happens to us that is not foretold somehow in

81

a dream. And invariably, this dream also prepares us or in some way suggests what we must do about a forthcoming event.

When the event foretold by a dream is either disagreeable or tragic, it is as if the unconscious were telling us by means of the dream that we should be strong and prepare ourselves for a disastrous occurrence. What seems to take place then is a strengthening of the mental and emotional aspect of an individual. Because he or she has already lived the negative experience in a dream, he/she is better prepared to face it in reality. In this sense we could say that the prophetic dream cushions an individual against sudden shocks that could be threatening to his/her physical and mental well-being. Likewise, exciting or joyous events are often foretold in dreams because they can also be taxing emotionally and physically to an individual.

How to Handle Bad Dreams

First of all, we must try to determine if the bad dream was the result of a heavy meal ingested just before going to sleep. If this was not the case, we can then proceed to identify the dream motifs and try to interpret their symbolism. If we discern a message in the dream symbols we can then try to adopt whichever protective measures we can, if there are any. If there are none, we should then try to relax and take the dream at face value.

It is simply useless to worry about a bad dream because we can never tell which ones are prophetic and which ones are simply an expression of negative trends in our mental makeup. And in any case, the prophetic dream can seldom be averted. It simply foretells something that is going to happen and over which we have no control.

How to Recall Your Dreams

It has been ascertained under laboratory conditions that everyone dreams for at least one hour each night, although this hour is not continuous but rather composed of dream segments of varying lengths.

Because dreams are remembered only if the dreamer wakes up during a dream (the REM period), or within ten minutes from the moment he or she awakes, it is not easy to recall every dream we have during the night. Sometimes we cannot recall any dreams in detail, although we are vaguely aware of having had a dream.

Perversely, dreams seem to grow more vague and difficult to remember the harder we try to recall them.

So how do we capture the elusive memory of a dream? Simpy by telling ourselves each night we want to remember our dreams upon awakening and by keeping a dream record.

Your Dream Record

It is not difficult to keep a dream record. All that is needed is a large notebook (kept specially for that purpose) and determination. The notebook must be kept by the bedside, and each dream that is remembered immediately upon awakening should be written down in every detail. It is important that dreams are recorded before getting out of bed, as they tend to fade with every waking thought.

If one awakens in the middle of the night after a particularly vivid dream, that dream should be noted down immediately instead of waiting until the next morning. To wait invariably means losing the dream. This happens because in the course of the night we will have several other dreams superimposing on the one we did not record, with the result that they will erase all memory of that particular dream.

It is important to jot down next to each dream the date when it was recorded and the general feelings it awoke in the individual. Usually the feelings left in a person by a dream are an indication of the inner conflicts faced by his/her unconscious and the type of message it is trying to seep through to the conscious personality. For this reason, it is helpful to identify these feelings as we record the dream, and set them down underneath the dream record as a commentary.

Dream Analysis

We said earlier that our dreams are symbolic images released by the unconscious mind during sleep. We also said that we can control these images in a variety of ways, such as mental suggestion. However, these images cannot be implanted in the unconscious unless they belong to the individual's actual experience. For example, you cannot expect to dream of the Champs Elysees in all its glory if you have never been to Paris. In other words, the unconscious can only work with material that has been stored within it through previous experience.

Dream Motifs

We mentioned earlier the symbols that reoccur in everyone's dreams and which Jung called dream motifs. Examples of the dream motifs are dreams about trains, weddings, flying, climbing, falling and hundreds of other subjects. These are the dreams that compose the typical dream dictionaries, such as the one included in this book.

When we analyze a dream we must try to identify as many motifs as there are in the dream. So if we dream we are running down a flight of stairs in the pursuit of a thief who has just stolen our wallet, we should be able to identify four motifs: 1. Running downstairs; 2. Pursuit; 3. Thief; and 4. Wallet.

We then find the traditional meanings associated with each of these motifs as given in a dream dictionary.

Next, we concentrate on each motif and write down the first thing that comes to our minds in connection with that particular subject. This will reveal to us what individual meaning each motif has for us. This meaning may vary from one person to another.

Also to be taken into consideration during dream analysis is the immediate environment of the dreamer, and any specific problems or personal conflicts he or she may be facing when he/she has a dream. Obviously, it cannot mean the same thing to dream about a waterfall if you live near Niagara than if you live near the Mohave desert. Likewise, it will not mean the same thing to have violent dreams if you are a policeman or a gangster than if you are a priest or a nun. Therefore, a person's immediate surroundings, his or her moods and his/her personal life will be reflected somehow in his/her dreams, and for this reason they should be considered during dream analysis.

You should make a habit of recording the actual experiences you associate with certain dream motifs or symbols. For example, if you discover that shortly after dreaming of a rose you get a letter with pleasant news, you should record this experience, and take it into consideration whenever you see roses in your dreams. If you are careful in the compilation of your dream record, it should not be very long before you have put together your very own dream dictionary that applies only to you.

The Sleep Ritual

Most of us go to sleep every night too tired or sleepy to follow any given ritual. We take our sleeping habits for granted, as well as our dreams. But, in reality, our sleeping periods are every bit as important as our waking periods because during sleep we adjust to and assimilate the conflicts we face during our waking time. This is done, as we have seen, through the symbology of dreams. It is, therefore, very important to go to sleep every night in the proper frame of mind. A short sleep ritual is the best way to accomplish this, and all of us, no matter how tired or how busy, can find the time to conduct such a ritual. It does not take very long, and the difference can change our lives.

The sleep ritual suggested here is quite simple. The first thing to do once you are in bed and ready to go to sleep is to lie flat on your back with eyes closed and arms resting alongside your body, starting with your feet and moving upward slowly until you have relaxed the muscles of your head and scalp. While you are relaxing each group of muscles you should be breathing deeply and evenly.

When your body feels comfortable and relaxed, you should proceed to implant in your unconscious whatever suggestion you desire to take place during your dreams. At this point, you should tell yourself that you wish to remember all important dreams upon awakening and that you will not be afraid of any dream you may have, no matter how disagreeable. This is all you need to do. It is simple, easy and short, but you will feel the difference in the positive quality of your next dreams. Because some people may fall asleep during the relaxation and deep breathing period, some psychologists recommend implanting your suggestions first and then proceeding with the muscle relaxation.

If you wish to contact someone on the unconscious level during sleep, you can do it also at the time of your sleep ritual by simply stating your intention to meet this person during your sleep and seeing the outcome of the meeting in a dream.

Remember at all times that dreams are not only messages but also accurate records of the state of your unconscious mind. Their main purpose is to make your life easier and more bearable, and to give you more control over your destiny. By understanding your dreams, you will not only understand yourself better but will also understand others and their relationship to you.

Through proper dream analysis your horizons will expand and your chances of success will increase a hundredfold. We have shown you how to achieve these goals. Put the acquired knowledge to good use, and may you have many happy dreams.

Dream Dictionary

NOTE: This dream dictionary gives the traditional or fixed meaning for each dream motif listed. The personal conditions of the dreamer and his or her immediate environment must also be taken into consideration. The numbers following each dream motif and their meaning are those ascribed to the dream by popular tradition, and are believed to be lucky in games of chance.

—A—

A—Business success. 1, 10

Abandonment—Difficulties and personal conflicts; may also indicate a need for independence. It is important to note what is being abandoned and by whom, as these things or individuals may be leaving the dreamer's life soon. 8, 80

Abdomen—If the abdomen looks normal, you will realize your fondest wishes. If it is bleeding or unhealthy, ou may be facing unhappiness soon. Beware of accidents. 3, 37

Abortion—Foretells incoming poor health. In a woman's dream, it warns her of a bad decision that she is about to make, which could result in great unhappiness. 9, 93

Abscess—The dreamer has a problem he or she refuses to acknowledge. He/she must be brave and resolve the situation, even if sorrow is involved. If he/she does, he/she will overcome all obstacles. 7, 87

Abuse—If somebody is abusing the dreamer, he or she will be faced with the enmity and persecution of false friends. If the dreamer is abusing someone, he/she will be unfortunate in his/her business affairs. 15, 8

Abyss—Dangers, threats, misfortune which you may or may not be able to overcome. If you fall into the abyss, you will be faced with many difficulties of a personal nature. This dream may also foretell death to the dreamer. If the dreamer does not fall, but descends into the abyss, it is an indication of the need to search into the unconscious for solutions to personal problems. 11, 14, 69, 70, 75

Acceptance—To dream that a business proposition has been accepted means that the dreamer will succeed in making a trade that he or she fears will be a failure. To dream of being accepted by a lover foretells much happiness with that person and a possible wedding. 5, 57

Accident—The dreamer should avoid traveling for some time as his or her life may be in danger. 98, 91

Accordion—To hear the music of an accordion foretells amusements and pleasantries to come. To play the accordion portends that the dreamer will win the love of his or her sweetheart through an unhappy event. 4, 8, 18

Accusation—Denotes quarrels to come, as well as scandals. 3, 10, 39

Aches—Someone may be profiting from your ideas. May also foretell heartbreak through an inconstant lover. This dream also warns the dreamer against chills and possible illness. 6, 62

Acid—To drink it denotes anxiety to come. To see it foretells treachery being planned against you. 42, 86

Acorn—This dream foretells much joy and success

to the dreamer. Gains and plenty should be forthcoming soon. To eat them indicates the rise from an obscure position to one of authority and fame. 19, 97

Acquit—To dream one is acquitted of a crime foretells the acquisition of valuable property which may be entangled in legal troubles. 28, 41

Actor and Actress—To see either one in a dream foretells much pleasure to come. If you are in love with one, you will not work hard for your money. If the actor or actress is dead in real life, you will be faced with hardships. 14, 36, 52

Adder—Foretells deceit and treachery. You have a hidden enemy. 98, 82, 11

Admiration—If you dream you are admired, you will have good fortune. If you admire someone else, you will soon face difficulties. 59, 71

Adoption—To dream that either you or another is adopting a child means you will be making fortunate changes around you. 21, 40

Adultery—If you commit adultery in a dream, your marriage may not be as solid as it seems. This dream denotes dissatisfaction and the desire to change. 1, 11, 39

Adventure—The desire to travel, to see new faces and do new things. New changes of a positive nature are coming into the life of the dreamer. 10, 91

Adversary—If you overcome the adversary, you will escape some forthcoming disaster. Dream foretells that the dreamer is his or her worst enemy and could be to blame in a coming conflict. 5, 11, 50 55

Advertisement—If you read one, you are in danger of being overcome by enemies. 27, 64

Advice—To receive it, denotes your outlook in life is improving and your overall situation will be better soon. To give it, you will be admired and respected by many people.

Afraid—To be afraid in a dream denotes anxieties brewing beneath the surface which will soon have to be faced. It is a call from the unconscious to be strong and have faith in your own inner powers, as you can succeed if you only try. 75, 49

Africa—This dream denotes mystical experiences and love of nature. Expect the unexpected. 99, 35

Afternoon—A sunny afternoon foretells lasting and pleasant friendships will be made. If the afternoon is rainy and gray, sadness and disappointments will soon be forthcoming. 78, 65

Age—To dream of age foretells failures in your undertakings. To see oneself looking older denotes illness and unsatisfactory business deals. 66, 68

Agony—This dream portends a mixture of sorrows and pleasures. Beware of imaginary fears that will torture you without need. 98, 49

Air—If the air is clear, you will soon have good luck and fortune. If the air is fragrant, you will be successful in love affairs. Stale or foul air predicts illness and bad luck. 79, 18

Airplane—Unusual experiences and forthcoming good luck. 86, 75

Alabaster—Foretells a successful marriage and fortunate business deals. If an alabaster figure is broken, sorrows may be near. 20, 51

Alarm—This dream denotes secret fears and anxieties. Be careful while traveling and do not trust your personal affairs to anyone. 12, 30

Alimony—Responsibilities shunned. Financial difficulties approaching. 32, 61

Alligator—Be careful of hidden enemies and watch your general health and physical safety. If the alligator attacks and overcomes you, you are facing serious dangers. If you destroy it you will overcome all difficulties.

Almonds—Wealth and good fortune are in store for the dreamer. This good fortune, however, could soon be followed by sadness. 61, 76

Alms—If they are given or taken unwillingly, the dream portends bad luck to the dreamer. If they are well received, good fortune is soon forthcoming. 23, 60

Alone—Happiness in the future. 1, 4, 7

Altar—The dream warns against a serious mistake about to be made by the dreamer. It also foretells a sudden marriage to the dreamer. 79, 36, 51, 62

Aluminum—This dream denotes acceptance of one's fate. If the metal is tarnished it foretells unexpected sorrows. 29, 42

Ambassador—This dream foretells misfortune and hasty news. 63, 65, 72

Ambition—Denotes health, wealth and good fortune. 3, 31, 69

Ambulance—Rapid recovery from a forthcoming illness. 61, 17

Ambush—Danger is closer to you than you suspect. Be careful when walking the streets and while traveling. 98, 38

America—Many honors and success will be yours, but you will be beset by envy and hidden enemies. 48, 13

Amethyst—To see one in a dream portends contentment and success in business. If the amethyst is lost, beware of broken engagements and slighted love. 9, 57

Amorous—You should be careful in affairs of the heart, for they can bring you disgrace and scandals. 55, 37

Amputation—This dream denotes loss of property, especially pertaining to business. 10, 88

Amusement—To be in a place of amusement indicates illicit pleasures and unfaithfulness on the part of your lover. It also portends false friends and dangers while traveling. 8, 48, 58

Anchor—To see one signifies an assured future and hopes realized. But it also portends quarrels between lovers. Pleasant voyages to sailors. 39, 47, 56

Anchovies—Sorrows and troubles are forthcoming. 27, 92

Andirons—Good will among friends so long as there are burning logs in the fireplace. If the grate is empty, the dream denotes loss of property and death. 34, 43

Angel—This dream foretells you will receive happy news. If the angel does not approach you, it is a symbol that you should change your way of life. Beware of dangers. 14, 65

Anger—Difficult trials await you. You will be disappointed in love and enemies may attack you. If others are angry with you and you keep your composure, you will overcome a forthcoming difficulty. 16, 41, 44

Animals—To dream of many animals is a good omen for lovers and indicates a happy wedding. 4, 14, 44

Ankle—Someone will help you without your knowledge. 46, 71

Antiques—This dream portends a long and happy life for you and those you love. 99, 10

Ants—Petty annoyances and greed. General dissatisfaction in most things. 2, 7, 41

Anvil—If the anvil is being used and sparks are flying, the dream denotes arguments and disagreements among co-workers. Otherwise it portends pleasant work and much success to women. A broken anvil signifies wasted opportunities. 35, 37, 53

Anxiety—Strangely enough, this is a good omen indicating that threats and difficulties will be overcome by the dreamer. Success and good fortune should soon be forthcoming. 22, 38

Apartment—Beware of family arguments. 33, 41

Ape—Denotes illness and bad luck. Beware of deceit, as a false friend wants your downfall. 4, 5, 6, 31

Apology—Someone with whom you quarrelled will return to your life. 78, 52

Apparel—If the apparel is clean and pretty, the dreamer's undertakings will meet with success. If soiled or ragged, poverty and ill luck are near. The

color of the clothes one sees in a dream are important, as they are symbolic of the dreamer's state of
mind. Happy, bright colors denote positive thoughts
and optimism. Dark or drab colors signify pessimism
and anxiety. 4, 13

Apparition—Be careful with your children and all
those who depend on you, as danger threatens
them. Both life and property may be in danger.
20

Applause—Beware of vanity and arrogance, as they
may prove your undoing. 86, 15

Apples—Your hopes will be realized. This is an
excellent omen signifying peace, prosperity and
good fortune. Only if the apples are rotten or green
or imperfect in any way is the dream a bad omen. In
this case, the dream portends all your present plans
will meet with failure. 4, 11, 44

Apprentice—To serve as an apprentice means you
will have to struggle to win a place among your
peers. 1, 36, 46

Apricots—To see them growing denotes that the
future will not turn out to be as rosy as it now may
seem. But to eat apricots denotes good fortune. 28,
40, 78

April—Much happiness and pleasure should be
forthcoming. If the weather is bad, it signifies the
passing away of ill luck. 44, 74

Apron—Many pleasures in store for you. Also good
news. To a woman it is an indication of forthcoming
marriage. 4, 26

Arab—This dream portends business success and
traveling in foreign lands. It also denotes dangerous

and treacherous enemies. 66, 37

Arch—You will rise to fame and distinction through hard work and determination. If you pass through one, your company will be sought by those who disdained you in the past. A fallen arch signifies hopes destroyed. 17, 39

Archbishop—You will meet many obstacles on your road to success, but you will overcome them. 2, 7, 34

Architect—A change in your business may result in losses. To a woman it denotes she will not succeed in her marriage plans. 4, 8, 48

Argue—You will have a long life with great business success. 37, 65

Arm—Troubles and interference from others between husband and wife. Beware of treachery and deceit from those around you. 16, 8, 90

Army—Troubles and difficulties in the family. You will need much strength and determination to overcome obstacles, but you will succeed. 9, 83, 12

Aroma—To a woman it denotes she will soon be the recipient of the love of a fine man. For men it indicates pleasures and personal satisfactions. 77, 55, 9

Arrest—Your present troubles will soon be dissipated and followed by happiness. 78, 41, 20

Arrow—Pleasures and joys to follow. Pleasant trips will soon be undertaken. If the arrow is old or broken, it signifies sorrows in love. 75, 31, 2

Artist—Success in all your dealings through good taste and diplomacy. 6, 96, 14

Ascent—If you ascend to the top, you will meet with success after much struggle. If your ascent stops before reaching the top, you will have many obstacles to overcome which may prove too powerful and insurmountable. Keep trying and success may be yours. 88, 4, 28

Ashamed—Your business will prosper. Much success coming your way. 72, 93, 1

Ashes—This signifies sorrows and many unhappy changes in your life, especially in your love life. Also portends sorrows through children. 35, 5, 16

Asia—Changes to come but with no material benefits. 62, 97, 4

Asp—Hidden enemies will try to cause havoc in your life. Sorrows in love affairs and unforeseen calamities. 2, 15, 63

Asparagus—Prosperous surroundings and obedient children. If it is eaten, much success in business ventures. 12, 10, 1

Ass—If it is carrying a burden, you will succeed after much toil and hardship. Beware not to be used by others. 31, 8, 72

Assassin—If you are his victim, you will not succeed in your undertakings. This dream is a warning against losses through hidden enemies. 88, 94, 13

Assistance—To give it denotes you will succeed in your efforts to rise to a higher position. If it is given to you, you will have the help of loving friends. 76, 5, 59

Astrology—Your future is full of unexpected pleasures and success. 19, 90

Asylum—Sickness and poor business deals. 44, 82

Athlete—You will be faced with many family arguments. Do not let them upset you unduly, as they will pass. 29, 41, 1

Atlas—To look at one denotes you will study every proposition with care before making a decision. 79, 9, 14

Attic—You have certain hopes that will not materialize through lack of solid basis. You will solve all your problems through careful reasoning. 6, 36, 13

Attorney—Your friends will cause you more worries than your enemies. Disputes of a serious nature will arise unexpectedly. 10, 7

Auction—Bright prospects in your business deals. To dream you buy objects at an auction denotes good luck to tradesmen and farmers. Plenty at the table for the housewife. 18, 75, 3

August—Unfortunate business deals and difficulties in love. To dream you are married in this month denotes sorrows in your married life. 76, 41, 4

Aunt—You will be severely criticized for your actions. 32, 92, 8

Aura—This dream denotes mental unrest and the desire to find peace within. 9, 11, 71

Australia—A total change in your life should soon be forthcoming. 37, 52, 9

Author—If an author dreams his or her manuscript is rejected by a publisher, it denotes that after initial doubts his/her work will be accepted and published successfully. 69, 73, 7

Automobile—If you are driving one, you are in control of your life. If someone is doing the driving and you are a passenger, the car driver also controls or directs your life in some way. 7, 64, 96

Autumn—You will acquire property through the efforts of someone who cares deeply for you. To dream of marrying in autumn means you will have a happy married life. 55, 75, 7

Avocado—You will be visited by someone you are very fond of. 76, 31, 6

Awake—If you dream you are awake, you will have unusual experiences that will leave you depressed and unhappy.

Axe—You will have to struggle for all your accomplishments. For a woman this dream means her future husband will be kind and pleasant, but not rich. A broken axe indicates illness and money losses. 13, 42, 6

—**B**—

Baby—If the baby is crying, illness and disappointments are forthcoming. A happy baby means love returned and many loving friends. If you are nursing the baby, deceits and treachery from those you trust most. 8, 54, 37

Bachelor—To a man, the dream denotes he will have difficulties with women. To a woman, that she will have a love affair with a married man. Loss of honor to politicians. 13, 2, 86

Backgammon—Your friends will turn their backs on you through no fault of your own. This dream denotes afflictions and conflicts. 88, 6, 49

Bacon—To eat it is good luck for you and those close to you. Rancid bacon denotes poor perception and bad judgment in your affairs. 33, 9, 2

Bag—You will have to work hard for your money, but success will be yours after some struggles. 22, 4, 81

Bagpipe—Happy news should be coming soon, but you should be careful with your money. 30, 82, 8

Bail—If you are looking for someone to bail you out in a dream, you will be faced with unexpected difficulties, and accidents are possible. If you bail another, you will still face some bad luck, but not as bad. 29, 87

Bake—A bad dream for a woman. It portends pregnancy, often unwanted. Poverty and ill luck. 2, 40

Balcony—This dream portends separation for lovers. Also bad news from friends or relatives. 8, 61

Baldness—If you see a baldheaded man in a dream, you will have troubles with crooked people in your business. If you see a bald woman instead, you will have a quarrelsome wife (if a man) and will dominate your husband (if a woman). 10, 97

Ball—You have many good friends who appreciate and respect you. Good times are forthcoming soon. 99, 1

Ballet—Unfaithfulness in your married life, either on your part or on that of your spouse. Quarrels between lovers. 15, 6

Balloon—Hopes not realized. Failures in all types of business. 33, 71

Banana—This dream portends an unhappy choice of marriage partner. Struggles in married life and bad financial decisions. 29, 6

Banjo—Many amusements and pleasant times are coming. 35, 2

Bank—If you see empty teller windows, you will suffer money losses. If a teller gives you money, your business will prosper. If you see large amounts of money in a bank, you will achieve much wealth and prosperity. 88, 70

Banquet—A good dream that indicates your friends will come to your aid when you need them. If you are partaking of a banquet, you will have great gains in your business and much happiness and success in all aspects of your life. 21, 9, 1

Baptism—A call for temperance and more restraint in your usual habits. 81, 11, 90

Bar—To attend one, you will engage in an illegal money-making scheme of dubious outcome. 83, 96

Barber—Success and good fortune will come after hard work. 7, 41

Barefoot—Your expectations will come to naught, and you will have to overcome many difficulties. 20, 66

Barking—You should listen to the advice of close friends, as they mean you well and know what they are talking about. 57, 43

Barn—If the barn is full of grain and healthy animals are near, you can expect great prosperity and happiness. If the barn is empty, you will face poor finances and lack of funds. 44, 68

Barrel—If it is full, you will enjoy great wealth. If it is empty, poverty may be your future lot. 87, 38

Baseball—You will be very popular among your friends because of your easygoing ways and charm. 31, 97

Basement—If you descend to one, you will need to search within yourself for a solution to your problems. If you are trapped in one, you will find yourself in a rut with very few opportunities to advance. 98, 59

Basket—If you see or carry a basket, you will meet with much success, so long as the basket is full. An empty basket, however, indicates forthcoming hardships. 66, 70

Bat—You will toil hard and long, but you will eventually meet with success. 74, 80

Bath—If the dreamer is young, he or she is very infatuated with someone who is not totally responsive to his or her feelings. For a pregnant woman, this dream warns against a possible miscarriage. A warm bath is an indication of negative influences around the dreamer. 88, 17, 4

Bats—To dream this dreaded creature denotes dangers and ill luck. The death of parents or friends is indicated, as well as the danger of losing a limb or the eyesight. A white bat is a sure omen of death, often that of a child. 42, 89

Battle—Struggles against personal conflicts, but with eventual success. If you are defeated in battle, it denotes you will suffer through the mistakes of others. 36, 98

Bayonet—You will be in danger of being defeated by enemies, unless you are holding the bayonet. In this latter case, your chances of success are better, but you are still facing the same dangers. 76, 48

Beads—People in high circles will distinguish you with their friendship. If you count the beads, you will have much happiness and good luck. 28, 60

Beans—This dream portends a contagious illness. If the beans are dried, you will face many disappointments in your affairs. 33, 79

Bear—To a woman, this dream indicates rivalries and general misfortunes. To kill a bear means freedom from present troubles. In general the dream foretells strong competition that you will not find easy to overpower. 64, 14

Beard—You will have financial difficulties. To a woman, this dream forewarns against an unwise marriage. 78, 58

Beauty—Pleasures and satisfaction in your business deals. A beautiful child foretells a happy union. 77, 55

Bed—You will be faced with a change of residence soon. If bed is clean and fresh-looking, you will soon solve your most pressing problems. 32, 14

Bedroom—You will travel to foreign lands and will enjoy the company of pleasant friends. 55, 3

Beef—Beware of accidents and bruises and scrapes. If the meat is bloody or raw, the danger of cancerous tumors is forewarned. If meat is cooked, much affliction and sorrow, with the possible loss of life through tragic events. If the beef is served pleasantly and in good company, these evil portents are cancelled and the dream then signifies harmony in love and business. 77, 88

Beer—If you drink it at a bar, many disappointments. If others drink it, hidden enemies are planning your downfall. 62, 18

Bees—Many pleasant and profitable business deals. Much happiness through loving children. If the bee stings, you will suffer losses or injuries from a friend. 52, 61

Beetles—You will be faced with bad luck, but you will overcome in the long run and enjoy some financial success. 10, 72

Beets—Happiness in love affairs. Good tidings if you eat them in the company of others. 23, 13

Beggar—You will soon face a change of fortune that will bring you many financial gains. 56, 29

Bells—If they toll, you will hear of the death of distant friends. If you see the Liberty Bell, you will enjoy dominion over your enemies. 92, 23, 16

Belly—To see a swollen belly indicates a serious illness. A healthy belly denotes unhealthy desires. 68, 88

Belt—You will soon meet someone who will bring you many misfortunes. 74, 18

Bench—If you sit on one, have no confidence in debtors and a certain close friend. If others sit on one, happy reunions with friends from whom the dreamer has been separated through misunderstandings. 93, 71

Bet—Take care in all new undertakings lest you

make a wrong decision. 66, 36

Bible—Some unexpected event will bring you much happiness and peace of mind. 99, 75

Bicycle—You will soon be facing an important decision. If you ride it downhill, beware of scandals and ill health. If uphill, you will soon be facing bright prospects. 62, 7, 25

Billiards—Troubles are soon to come. Lawsuits and slander will cause you much grief. 83, 80

Birds—Flying birds denote joy and prosperity. A wounded bird is a symbol of coming sorrows through offspring. 33, 12

Birth—You will find your social enjoyment overshadowed by unexpected sorrows. 29, 81

Birthday—This is an omen of poverty and ill luck for the young and old alike. 58, 80

Biscuits—You will make a journey that will prove profitable for you and yours. 61, 46

Bishop—Great mental worries and complicated business deals. Hard work and many illnesses. 60, 16

Bite—You have much work ahead of you that you should not postpone if you can help it. You may suffer losses through an enemy. 92, 37

Black—Many difficult times ahead. 8, 13

Blackboard—If you see writing on it, you will hear of the illness of a relative or close friend; also indicates financial reverses. 14, 86

Blacksmith—Hard work will soon bring you well-earned success and improved finances. 91, 55

Bladder—Forthcoming joys and success. 7, 90

Blanket—You should use caution and watch your

health in order to avoid an illness. 68, 66

Blasphemy—Ill luck and troubles in all your affairs. 80, 48

Blind—If you are blind in the dream, you are missing good business opportunities through poor judgment; also someone is taking advantage of your good will. If somebody else is blind, someone will come to you for advice. 12, 54

Blood—A severe disappointment will bring you much unhappiness. Beware of unusual friends and guard your health. 99, 89

Blossoms—You will meet with much success and peace of mind in the near future. 77, 17

Blows—Beware of physical injury, especially to the head. Be careful while traveling. 68, 15

Blue—You will have much prosperity through the efforts of others. 62, 53

Boa—Ill luck and many conflicts in all aspects of your life. Be careful with your physical and mental health, and beware of enemies at work against you. To kill it denotes triumph over evil. 89, 18

Boat—You will achieve all your aims in life, so long as the boat sails on clear waters. If the water is unsettled, unhappy changes threaten the dreamer. 98, 80

Bones—To see them protruding from the flesh, treachery is at work against you. To see a pile of bones denotes poverty and even hunger around you, as well as the threat of contaminants in your immediate environment. 87, 46

Books—Honors and riches if you dream you are studying them. To see your book being printed is a warning against possible losses in your business. 12, 73

Boots—To wear them, you will have good luck in all your dealings. If the boots are old or torn, you will be facing illness and dangers. If another wears the boots, someone will take your place in your lover's affections. 57, 27

Bottle—You will soon enjoy a love conquest. Prosperity and success will soon be yours. 37, 91

Bouquet—A bright and beautiful bouquet denotes a legacy from a wealthy and unknown relative. If flowers are dry, the dream denotes death and sickness. 85, 56

Bow and Arrow—Difficulties in getting others to carry out your instructions, with dire results. If you hit the bullseye, you will overcome all problems and have many financial and personal gains. 9, 76

Bowling—You will realize your fondest wishes. 57, 19, 10

Box—Many pleasures through traveling so long as box is not empty. If it is, beware of disappointments, A box full of money indicates a pleasant, early retirement. 75, 91

Boy—Your family will grow through a welcome addition. 1, 90

Bracelet—This is an indication of an early marriage. 31, 49

Brain—If you see the brains of animals, you may face mental distress. If you see your own brain, you are unhappy in your immediate surroundings. If you eat brains, you will gain knowledge and profit from it. 43, 27

Branch—If it is full of fruit and green leaves, you will enjoy wealth and prosperity. If it's dry, sad news from someone far away. 18, 32

Brandy—You will enjoy a happy love affair. 21, 62

Brassiere—Someone else is enjoying what you desire most. 7, 13

Bread—To eat it means wealth and personal satisfaction. To see and smell freshly baked bread indicates freedom from financial worries. 61, 74

Breakfast—To see it indicates hasty, favorable news. To eat it means you may soon fall into a trap. 23, 47

Breast—If it is full and well formed, you will soon enjoy good fortune. If it is shriveled or ill formed, you will have many disappointments in love. 55, 70

Breath—If breath is sweet, you will enjoy respectability and the admiration of others. If it is fetid, beware of illness and traps. Shortness of breath denotes lost opportunities. 31, 63

Bribe—You will receive payment for some money you loaned a friend. 42, 79

Brick—Unsettled business and lovers' quarrels. To make bricks denotes failure in making a fortune. 84, 24

Bride—You will inherit money unexpectedly if you see yourself as a bride. To kiss one means reconciliation between friends. If she kisses you, you will enjoy good health and the love of a wealthy person. 55, 97

Bridge—To cross it safely, the overcoming of difficulties. To see it falling down, beware of treacherous people around you. 16, 38

Bridle—You will engage in a dubious business but you will succeed in the end. 39, 40

Brimstone—This dream denotes that through shady dealings you will lose many friends and business contacts. There is danger of a contagious disease or air pollutants in your vicinity. 89, 68

Bronchitis—Discouraging prospects are ahead for you. Also foretells setbacks through a serious family illness. 68, 96

Bronze—A bronze statue denotes you will fail in your efforts to win the affections of the one you love. If the statue moves, you will have a love affair with that person but will not marry him or her. To see the bronze metal means unsettled business affairs. 73, 62

Broom—You will make rapid progress in your road to success. 2, 45

Broth—This dream denotes sincerity in your friends. They will help you in every way they can. You will enjoy a lasting and happy love affair. To make it means you will control both your destiny and that of another. 9, 12

Brothel—You may encounter difficulties through your material indulgences. 15, 8

Brother—You may expect violent quarrels with relatives or close friends. 43, 14

Brother-in-law—This dream signifies that relatives take advantage of you. 45, 67

Brown—This color denotes a state of depression and confusion in your general affairs. If someone else wears that color, he or she feels unhappy about his or her relationship with you. 44, 84

Brush—To dream of using one means you will suffer misfortune through your mismanagement of your own affairs. If the brush is old, it denotes sickness and ill health. To see many brushes signifies you will work at various jobs with financial rewards. 91, 32

Buckle—You will receive many invitations to parties and places of amusement. 16, 20

Bugs—Complications in your daily life. Sickness in the family is foretold. 86, 98

Building—If you see an attractive building in a dream, you will enjoy a long and fruitful life, with much traveling and many pleasures. If the building is dilapidated, you should beware of ill health and losses in love and business. 76, 54

Bull—If it pursues you, beware of coming business troubles. If it looks tame and healthy, you are in control of your life. 92, 16

Burglar—You have dangerous enemies to contend with. If your home is being burglarized, your standing in the community will be assailed, but you will triumph in the end. 28, 64

Burial—If the sun is shining during the burial, it indicates a forthcoming wedding and good health for the dreamer and his or her immediate family. If it is raining, sickness and bad news will soon come. 58, 50

Buried alive—You will soon make a grave mistake that will be turned against you by your opponents. If you are rescued, you will win at the end. 64, 47

Burns—Good news should be soon forthcoming. If you burn yourself, it denotes learning through mistakes to your advantage. 61, 19

Butcher—There may be a long and fatal illness in your family. Be careful of what you write in a letter or document, as it may be used later on to your detriment. 26, 30

Butter—If butter looks fresh and golden, you will enjoy good health and success through patient planning. 23, 62

Butterfly—This dream indicates prosperity and good fortune. If you see them flying, it denotes pleasant news from distant friends or relatives. To a woman, it foretells a faithful lover who will make her a fine husband. 55, 75

Buttocks—You can expect good fortune and success in the near future. 60, 71

Buttons—If they are shiny, it denotes the affection and respect of an attractive and wealthy marriage partner. If dull or rusty, they foretell ill health and steady losses. To lose a button foretells business losses. 10, 35

Buzzard—Beware of accidents and losses. Also denotes slander and gossip will besmirch your character. 18, 48

—C—

Cab—You will try to keep a secret from your friends. If you drive it yourself, you will do manual labor with little chance of advancement. 13, 72

Cabbage—Many disorders in your life. If the cabbage is green, you will have love sorrows and infidelity in marriage. 58, 24

Cabin—Someone is plotting mischief against you. You may be entangled in a costly lawsuit. 30, 73

Cable—You will undertake hazardous work which will eventually result in many riches and happiness for you. If you receive a cablegram, you will soon be the recipient of disagreeable news. 49, 11

Cage—If birds are in the cage, you will enjoy great wealth and have many beautiful and charming children. If the cage is empty, someone will die in your immediate family. Caged, wild animals denote triumph over your enemies and personal victories. 88, 53

Cake—Your affections are well placed; your love will flourish and meet with happiness. Also, someone will leave you a home in his/her will. Good luck in all enterprises, so long as the cake is not a wedding cake. If it is, your luck will take a turn for the worse. 58, 94

Calendar—You should organize your affairs with greater care, as many unforeseen changes are forthcoming. 71, 34

Calves—If the calves are grazing on a green pasture, there will be many happy gatherings around you and much pleasure is in store for you. Wealth and prosperity will be forthcoming soon. 16, 25

Camel—You will find the patience and strength to overcome some forthcoming difficulties. To dream you own a camel indicates you will enjoy much wealth through mining property. 52, 76

Cameo—Sad events will soon take place either for you or someone close to you. 62, 49

Camera—To take pictures with one foretells disappointments in a close friend. 29, 56

Camp—A change in your affairs, as well as a long and tiresome journey. 38, 32

Campaign—To dream of a political campaign signifies originality of thought and determination to succeed. Also indicates victories over opponents. 7, 81

Canal—If the waters of the canal are muddy, the dream portends illness and stomach troubles. Clear waters indicate a peaceful and happy life to come. 36, 83

Canary—To hear one singing foretells unexpected pleasures and joys. For a young person to dream of owning one denotes academic honors and a literary career. If the canary dies, it portends unfaithfulness in close friends. 18, 73

Cancer—If the disease is cured in the dream, you will rise from poverty to much wealth. If the cancer is not cured, the dream denotes the illness of someone close to you and quarrels with loved ones. 63, 40

Candle—If you see one burning with a clear, bright flame, you can depend on the friendship of those around you and can expect good fortune in all your affairs. To snuff a candle portends the death of a close friend or relative. 37, 59

Candy—To dream you are making candy means you will make much profit from a small business. To dream of eating crisp, new candy denotes many social pleasures and lovemaking. Sour candy indicates illness and troubles with acquaintances. 95, 39

Cane—If you see one growing in a dream, you will have no difficulties in amassing a large fortune. 42, 61

Cannon—Both your home and possibly your country are in danger of illegal invasion and maybe a declaration of war. In general this dream portends struggles and defeat. 82, 60

Canoe—If you paddle a canoe on calm waters, you have enough confidence in yourself to triumph in your business deals. If you are in the company of your lover, you will marry soon and have a good marriage. Murky or turbulent waters indicate conflicts that will be difficult to overcome. 54, 47

Cap—You will take a part in some festivities. Any sport cap indicates a light outlook in life that will be of much help to you. 50, 25

Captain—To see one in a dream denotes you will realize your noblest aspirations. If a woman has this dream, she will be the victim of much jealousy and rivalry. 72, 49

Captive—If you see yourself captive, you will have

to deal with treachery. If you take someone else captive, you will associate with people of low moral caliber. 38, 58

Cards—If you see yourself playing cards you will realize your hopes, but only if you do not play for gain. If you play for stakes, you will find yourself in serious financial troubles. 65, 42

Carnival—You will soon engage in some unusual pastime or recreation. If masks are worn, there will be quarrels in the home and you will find your love unrequited. 78, 61

Carpet—To see one portends profits and wealthy friends. To walk on one means you will be prosperous and happy. 48, 72

Carpenter—You will work at an honest if humble trade, but will eventaully succeed in making a small fortune. 33, 40

Carriage—You will be making many visits. If you ride in one, you will be ill for some time, but not a serious illness. 98, 10

Carrot—To see one portends prosperity and good health. To eat it foretells an early marriage with a kind, loving person. 55, 2

Cartridge—Unhappy quarrels and disagreements. Unusual fate awaits you or someone close to you. 38, 58

Carving—If you carve a fowl, you will always have difficulties with your finances. To carve any other kind of meat denotes poor investments and business troubles. 69, 59

Cash—If you borrow some, you will find yourself in financial need if you do not curb your spending.

If you lend it, you will always be in comfortable financial conditions. 7, 40

Cask—It denotes prosperity and happy times to come, so long as it is full. If it is empty, your life will not be an easy one. 91, 11

Castle—If you are in one, you will have enough wealth to satisfy your every wish. You will travel extensively and meet people from many nations. 6, 50

Castor Oil—You distrust a friend who is sincere and trying to help you. 4, 82

Cat—This dream is an omen of bad luck unless you drive it away. If the cat attacks you, you have enemies who will seek your destruction. 9, 77

Caterpillar—You should not trust everyone around you because there are some people near you who are hypocritical and dangerous. The dream denotes a possible loss in love or business. 81, 44

Cathedral—You will long for the unattainable. If you enter the cathedral, you will achieve great things and enjoy the company of wise and faithful friends. 88, 1

Cattle—Fat and healthy cattle indicate prosperity and happiness through a pleasant and kind companion. If the cattle is lean and undernourished, you will probably work hard all your life because of your dislike of petty details. The dream is a warning to change your habits, if you wish to succeed. 5, 99

Cave—Many doubts will confuse you and cloud your judgment. Work and physical health are threatened. If you enter one, you may expect unexpected changes in your life. You will probably be separated from those you love and have difficulties in meeting them again. 60, 3

Celery—If the celery is crisp and green, you will be prosperous and happy in all your undertakings. If it is rotten or decaying, there may soon be a death in your family. To eat it denotes much love will be given you from friends and relatives. 20, 7

Cell—It would be better if you kept to yourself for a short period, as you need time to make an important decision. 8, 44

Cellar—You will have many doubts and lose confidence in your own abilities. You must endeavor to strengthen your will in order to succeed. 66, 90

Cemetery—Someone will recover from a desperate illness. If the cemetery is old and abandoned, your loved ones will leave you. To a bride, this dream portends widowhood. 80, 31

Chains—Unjust burdens will soon be heaped upon your shoulders. If you succeed in breaking away from them, you will free yourself from an unpleasant obligation. 13, 47

Chair—You will fail to meet an important duty. If you see someone sitting motionless in a chair, you will soon hear news of that person's death. 8, 71

Chalk—If you use the chalk, you will attain public honors. If you hold it in your hands, you are in for a setback in your personal affairs. 48, 10

Champagne—You will meet disappointments in your love affairs. 6, 52

Chandelier—Unexpected success will make it possible for you to attain your fondest dreams. If the chandelier is broken or dirty, you will make injudicious speculations that will cost you much money. 22, 80

Charcoal—If the charcoal is unlit, poverty and unhappiness are near. If the coals are red with fire, your life will succeed beyond your wildest expectations in the near future. 99, 7

Check—To receive one means you will receive some money or an inheritance. To pay out checks portends depression and business losses. 8, 62

Checkers—If you are playing checkers, you will have serious troubles and strangers will influence your life. If you win the game, you will succeed in some dubious business venture. 17, 4

Cheese—To eat it denotes serious disappointments. 20, 39

Cherries—You will gain popularity through your good will and kindness to others. To eat them means you will possess a much-wanted object. 63, 51

Chess—To play it denotes stagnation in business and poor health. If you lose the game, you will have many worries. If you win, you will overcome all troubles. 99, 27

Chest—You will have arguments with members of your family. 79, 23

Chestnuts—Business losses, but a pleasant companion for life. To eat them denotes passing troubles. 31, 62

Chickens—To see them denotes you will have worries for some time to come, but you will overcome them in the end. Young chicks indicate fortunate enterprises. To eat them denotes selfishness and unhappy love affairs. 88, 37

Children—To see beautiful children indicates prosperity and joy. To see a sick child indicates health for your children but worries of other kinds will beset you. 65, 32

Chimney—A disagreeable incident threatens your happiness. If fire is burning in a chimney, good fortune is approaching you. 9, 77

Chin—Your business affairs will improve in the future. 8, 19

China—To paint or arrange it denotes you will have a pleasant home and enjoy much comfort and pleasure through it. 5, 29

Chocolate—You will be a generous provider for those who depend on you. To see it, you will have pleasant companions and amusements. To drink it denotes prosperity after some difficult times. 34, 26

Choir—You may expect cheerful surroundings to replace your present discontent. To sing in a choir denotes unhappiness through the unfaithfulness of your lover. 12, 9

Choke—You will enjoy a long, pleasant life. 77, 35

Christ—To see Christ as a young child foretells many peaceful days to come, full of wealth and joy. If you see him in sorrow, you will long for distant loved ones and suffer from many unhappy events. 4, 71

Christmas Tree—Many joyful occasions and good fortune to come. 6, 22

Church—Disappointments in pleasures anticipated.

To enter a gloomy church denotes you will take part in a funeral. 82, 49

Cider—To see other people drinking it denotes you will be under the influence of false friends. To drink it yourself indicates you may overcome all obstacles if you are only willing to work harder. 51, 72

Cigar or Cigarette—New plans are soon to be made. All your expectations will be fulfilled with much happiness in your future. 3, 41

Circle—You will accomplish much less than you expect in your business or profession. 77, 49

Circus—You will meet with much unhappiness in the future. 6, 30

Cistern—You are in danger of a sudden illness difficult to diagnose. If cistern is empty, changes from joy to sorrow. 33, 76

City—If you dream of a strange city, you will change your mode of living and perhaps your residence. 6, 53

City Hall—Difficulties and possible lawsuits. To a woman, this dream portends a possible breakup with her lover. 59, 3

Clairvoyance—To dream of being clairvoyant denotes changes in your present occupation. To visit one foretells errors of judgment in your business that could prove costly. 18, 62

Clams—You will have deals with a stubborn but honest person. To eat them denotes you will enjoy someone else's prosperity. 90, 55

Clay—To dig up clay denotes you will have to submit to extraordinary demands on the part of an enemy. This dream is an evil omen for love affairs. 52, 14

Cliffs—Beware, for a large fire may destroy your property. 15, 48

Climb—You will achieve many honors and distinctions. 41, 35

Clock—This dream is a warning to beware of enemies nearby. If you hear one strike the hour, you will receive unpleasant news. The death of a friend may be near. 86, 20

Closet—Do not spend your money carelessly, for you could find yourself in bad economic straits soon. 33, 71

Clothes—Soiled or torn clothes indicate deceit and underhanded deals from strangers. Clean, new clothes indicate prosperity to come. 45, 52

Clouds—Dark, heavy clouds are an omen of difficulties to come. If rain is falling, the dream denotes illness and troubles. Bright clouds, with the sun shining through, indicate success after trouble. 24, 6

Clown—You will receive news of someone's death. 88, 44

Coat—To see a new coat denotes literary honors. To lose your coat portends you will have to rebuild your fortune after you lose it through mismanagement. An old, torn coat denotes the loss of a friend. 8, 27

Cock—To hear a cock crowing denotes a happy marriage. If cocks fight, you will leave your home because of family quarrels. 22, 1

Cocktail—This dream signifies loose living and dangers of moral depravity. 58, 15

Coconut—Your expectations are ill-placed. If coconut is dry, you will hear of the death of someone close to you. 17, 67

Coffee—To drink it denotes the disapproval of friends about your marriage intentions. If married, disagreements and quarrels are forthcoming. To see ground coffee foretells success in your struggles against troubles. 32, 6

Coffin—To farmers, this dream foretells blighted crops and unhealthy cattle. To businessmen, it denotes mounting debts. Death may follow shortly after this dream, but determination may overcome other bad omens. 66, 14

Coins—If they are made of gold, you will have great prosperity and will travel far. If they are made of silver, bad luck and family quarrels. If your lover gives you a silver coin, that person is planning to end the relationship. Copper or nickel coins denote ill luck and sorrows. 32, 56, 13

Cold—If you are suffering from a cold in a dream, you are warned to be careful of your affairs, for you will be facing underhanded deals from hidden enemies. Illness is also near. 82, 17

Collar—If you wear one, you will have high honors that you do not totally deserve. To a woman, the dream denotes she will have many admirers but not a lasting one. 75, 43

College—You will achieve the high position you desire. 4, 61

Collision—You will have a serious accident or business difficulties. For a woman, this dream denotes the inability to choose between two men, with disagreeable consequences. 11, 7

Comb—To dream of combing one's hair foretells the illness or death of a friend or relative. 9, 16

Comet—You will have unexpected troubles, but you will overcome them in the end. 13, 70

Compass—Loss and deception if it is pointed awry. Prosperity if it is used on board a ship. 99, 4

Compliment—You may soon be facing a family quarrel. 2, 49

Concert—Success in business and in love. The possibility of an inheritance is near. 66, 83

Confetti—If the confetti obstructs your view, you will lose much by procrastinating in your work for the sake of pleasure. 22, 8

Conspiracy—If you are the object of it, you will make an error in business that could prove costly. 84, 2

Convent—To be safe inside one denotes you will be protected from difficulties by your own foresight. If you meet a priest, you will meet also with sorrows in real life. 46, 17

Conversation—A long period of unexpected rain is forthcoming. 66, 5

Convict—Disaster and bad news. If you see yourself as a convict, you will have worries about personal afffairs. 73, 26

Cooking—If you cook a meal in a dream, you will be given some pleasant duty. If you use a cooking stove, you will lose a good friend through a disagreement. 37, 12

Copper—You will be oppressed by those in higher positions. 88, 61

Coral—Enduring friendship will be a solace in your

life. White coral foretells unfaithfulness in love. 58, 25

Cork—If you pop a cork on a bottle, the dream denotes prosperity and good luck to come. Medicine corks denote illness and hardships. 91, 28

Corn—To dream of husking corn indicates plenty and good fortune. If others gather the corn, you will rejoice in the good luck of someone dear. 55, 23

Corner—If you are hiding behind a corner, the dream is an evil omen, foretelling sorrows and dangers to come. Beware of someone you trust, who is a false friend. 9, 31

Cornet—If seen or heard, portends help from strangers. 45, 62

Corns—If you dream you have corns and they ache, beware of enemies undermining you. If you remove your corns, you will receive a large inheritance. 57, 20

Coronation—You will enjoy acquaintances with powerful people. 77, 27

Corpse—Bad news from distant loved ones. To see it in a coffin indicates trouble to the dreamer. 89, 40

Corset—You will quarrel with friends for petty reasons. 12, 4

Cotton—Successful business ventures. To see it ready for gathering denotes wealth and abundance for farmers. 33, 72

Couch—To recline on one denotes you will entertain false hopes. 72, 96

Counterfeit Money—You will have troubles with a worthless person. Bad times to come. 77, 46

Country—Good times are close at hand. If the country looks bare and dry, you will meet with difficult times. Famine and sickness may be near. 27, 14

Cousin—Disappointments and afflictions. If you dream of receiving a warm letter from a cousin, you will break relations with your family. 17, 15

Cows—To see cows with full udders denotes abundance and happiness. 35, 28

Crabs—Complications in your affairs. Also a long and difficult courtship for lovers. 2, 22

Cradle—If it is occupied by a lovely child, it portends prosperity and good fortune. If you rock your baby, serious illness in the family. 54, 61

Cream—You will be associated with wealthy people. To the farmer, it denotes good crops and pleasant family relationships. To drink it portends good fortune. 33, 13

Criminal—To associate with one denotes you will be troubled by unscrupulous people who will try to use you. To see one indicates you should beware of possessing other people's secrets lest they decide to silence you in order to ensure your silence. 88, 38

Cripple—To dream of being crippled denotes poverty and distress. Also difficulties in business. 6, 49

Cross—Troubles ahead. Be careful with your business deals. 9, 70

Crow—To see one means ill fortune to come. To hear one caw you will listen to bad advice and lose valuable business. 11, 57

Crowd—A well-dressed crowd denotes pleasant friends. A crowd in church signifies a death in the family. To see a crowd in the street denotes good business and prosperity. 7, 19

Crown—You will face new changes in your life and will travel far away from home. To wear one indicates loss of personal property. 88, 5

Crucifixion—Lost opportunities and false hopes. 12, 90

Crutches—You will depend largely on others for support and help. If you see others on crutches, you will labor in vain in the pursuit of wealth. 68, 39

Cry—Pleasures changing into gloomy prospects. 85, 60

Crystal—Depressions and conflicts in business and love. 77, 59

Cupid—You may expect good news. 72, 18

Curtains—Unwelcome visitors will cause you troubles. 9, 20

Cushion—If you recline on silken cushions, you will enjoy ease procured at others' expense. To see the cushions indicates you will have happiness in business and love. 5, 57

Cut—Sickness and a treacherous friend who will try to hurt you. 19, 67.

—**D**—

Daffodils—You will have luck in love. 75, 19, 1

Dagger—Threatening enemies. If you overcome

someone attempting to attack you with one, you will overcome an enemy. 17, 20

Daisy—Sadness if you see them in a bouquet. On a field, however, they denote happiness and radiant health. 8, 27

Dance—Pleasures and general happiness. If you are dancing in a dream, unexpected good fortune. 25, 37

Dandelion—Happy unions and prosperity. 79, 17

Dark—If darkness overtakes you, your work may not succeed. If sun shines through it, you will overcome all difficulties. This dream is a call to retain calm under stress. 66, 48

Dates—If they are still on the tree, prosperity and happy unions. To eat them prophesies difficult times to come. 37, 81

Daughter—Many unpleasant occurrences will give way to pleasure and happiness. 12, 73

Daughter-in-Law—Unusual event will affect your life soon, either for good or for bad, depending on the attitude of this relative in the dream. 76, 45

Day—Improvement in your personal life. If the day is cloudy, losses in business are indicated. 56, 46

Dead—Beware of coming troubles. If you see the dead well and happy, signifies you are letting wrong influences enter your life. 19, 62

Death—If any of your family is dead in a dream, you will experience sorrows in near future. 82, 39

Debt—Worries in business and love. 15, 29

Deer—Good friends will help you. To kill one denotes you are surrounded by unfriendly people. To hunt a deer denotes business losses. 70, 34

Dentist—You will have reason to doubt the sincerity of a so-called friend, if you see him working on your teeth. If he is working on someone else's mouth, you will be shocked by ugly gossip. 41, 17

Desert—To dream of walking through a lonely desert denotes poverty and racial uprisings. Great loss of life and property is threatened. 18, 49, 8

Desk—Unexpected luck will soon come your way. 23, 11, 32

Detective—Fortune and honors are soon forthcoming. This dream portends love troubles to women. 58, 29

Devil—To a farmer this dream denotes famine and death to his stock. To others it is a warning against unscrupulous people tempting you to break the law with the promise of big money. 77, 15

Diamonds—A very propitious dream denoting high honors and wealth. 12, 33

Dice—Unfortunate speculations, followed by poverty and despair. This dream is also an indication of a forthcoming epidemic. 86, 20, 6

Dictionary—To dream of one indicates you depend too much on the opinions of others. You should try making more decisions on your own. 80, 42

Digging—You will never want for anything, but your life will be an uphill struggle. 15, 32

Dinner—If you eat it alone, you will think before acting. If you eat dinner with your lover, it denotes you will quarrel and break up. 72, 45

Dirt—Fresh dirt around flowers indicates healthy surroundings and long life. If your clothes are soiled with dirt, you will be in danger of contagious diseases. 71, 41

Disease—Illness is near but of a short duration. You may have unpleasant arguments with a relative. 12, 59

Dish—Good fortune to touch them. If they break, bad luck to come, 29, 10

Diving—Beware of speculative ventures which may prove costly. 82, 40

Divorce—A warning that all is not well with your married life. If single, a break with your lover is imminent. 65, 73

Docks—Denotes an unpropitious journey which you should try to avoid. Accidents are possible. You should take care while driving and traveling. 85, 34

Doctor—An auspicious dream indicating good health and prosperity if you meet one socially. If you visit one professionally, serious illness for you or someone close to you. 21, 74

Dogs—A vicious dog indicates enemies and ill fortune. If he is friendly and licks your hand, you will have gains and sincere friends. 32, 43

Doll—Beware of light love affairs. You may cause trouble for yourself and someone else. 38, 54

Dominoes—If you lose while playing, you will be insulted by a friend. If you win, you will be much admired by low-class people. 52, 63

Donkey—If it brays, you will be insulted by a worthless person. If you ride one, you will travel to foreign lands and have many adventures. 32, 47

Door—To enter through one indicates slander. To

close one denotes protection against enemies. To see a closed door denotes lost opportunities. 9, 17

Dove—To see a pair building a nest indicates peace and joy to come. A dead dove means a separation between husband and wife or between lovers. 58, 13

Dragon—You allow yourself to be ruled by your passions. You must try to overcome your temper and violent nature. 78, 63

Dress—Troubles in your life through a scheming woman. 33, 13

Drink—To drink clear water denotes simple pleasures that will bring much joy to the dreamer. To drink liquor until one is overpowered by it indicates lack of self-control and danger of accidents. 54, 89

Driving—If the dreamer is doing the driving, he or she is in control of his/her life and should succeed in life. If someone else is driving, the dreamer is controlled by that individual. 79, 62

Drown—If you are drowning, you will suffer losses of business and property. To save others from drowning indicates you will help friends in need who will reward you amply later in life. 76, 24

Drugs—You will be surrounded by gossip and slander. Beware of false friends. 73, 48

Drum—To hear the beating of a drum denotes a distant friend is in need and wants your help. To see one denotes happy relationships with friends. 81, 93

Drunk—Financial difficulties and lack of self-control. 17, 26

Ducks—Wild ducks indicate fortunate journeys. To hunt them indicates loss of employment. To see them shot denotes that enemies are meddling in your affiars. 35, 74

Dust—Business losses through other people's faults. 82, 71

Dwarf—You will have unexpected problems at home which you will have difficulties overcoming. 33, 2

Dye—Unexpected changes in your life. Blue, red and gold dyes indicate prosperity. Black and gray foretell sorrows and bad luck. 11, 82

Dying—To see others dying foretells bad luck to you and those close to you. To see yourself dying portends that you are in danger of physical calamities through something or someone who is a source of pleasure. 88, 49

Dynamite—Many changes are coming into your life. 11, 46

—E—

Eagle—If one is flying high above you, it means lofty ambitions that will be realized. If it is poised on a high place, you will possess fame and fortune. To kill an eagle denotes no obstacle will ever be too difficult for you. 1, 10, 11

Ear—Someone is eavesdropping on you with the intention of learning enough about your affairs to be able to hurt you later. 98, 16

Earring—Good news and interesting work is before you. 20, 6

Earth—Momentous changes in your life is imminent. A move to another country is possible. 43, 29

Earthquake—Business failure and the possibility of wars between nations. 37, 71

Easter—Much happiness and joy are forthcoming. New hopes in a love that seems now lost. 7, 65

Eat—If you eat alone, you are facing losses and sadness. To eat with others denotes gains and good fortune which you will share with others. 23, 51

Ebony—Many distressing arguments in your home. 12, 30

Echo—Difficult times lie ahead. Beware of hasty decisions, especially in important matters. 34, 79

Eclipse—Temporary business difficulties, as well as family quarrels, if the eclipse is of the sun. If the moon is eclipsed, there is danger of contagious diseases or death. 48, 37

Egg—A nest of eggs indicates wealth and happiness, as well as a harmonious married life with many children. To eat eggs denotes unusual disturbances in the home. 44, 20

Elbow—Hard work ahead with small pay. For a woman, this dream indicates good marriage prospects. 9, 74

Electricity—Sudden changes around you which will not be for the best. If you are shocked by electricity, your life may be in danger. 61, 1

Elephant—Solid wealth will be yours, as well as high honors. You will have complete control of your business affairs and of your family life. 77, 18

Elevator—To ascend in one indicates you will soon rise to position and wealth. If you descend, you will face sadness and misfortune. 60, 81

Embrace—For lovers or married people, this dream foretells quarrels and disagreements. To embrace relatives indicates sickness is in store for them. 65, 36

Emerald—You will inherit property that will cause trouble with others. To buy one indicates unfortunate business deals. 15, 28

Emperor—To meet one indicates long trips that will not be pleasant or profitable. 38, 61

Employment—You are a very energetic person who likes to work. If you dream of an employer, you will soon change your line of work. 96, 30

Empress—You will receive high honors but pride will make you unpopular. 43, 82

Encyclopedia—You will seek literary honors that may cost you comforts and prosperity. 5, 91

Enemy—To dominate them denotes you will overcome business difficulties, enjoying wealth and prosperity as a result. If they overcome you, troubles and ill fortune may be near. 95, 20

Engagement—You will meet dishonest and insincere people. Be careful to whom you tell your troubles. 87, 52

Engineer—Tiresome journeys followed by pleasant reunions. 92, 23

Entrails—To see human entrails denotes misfortunes and unhappiness to come. Animal entrails indicate you will overcome a mortal enemy. 9, 17

Envy—You will make many friends through your warmth and care for others. If others envy you, you will be inconvenienced by the overzealousness of friends or relatives. 8, 67

Epidemic—Mental exhaustion is indicated and worries through disagreeable work. Contagious diseases are also possible. 41, 30

Escape—You will rise in the world through hard work and determination. If you try to escape and fail, you will suffer setbacks through dishonest people. 22, 49

Europe—You will travel to another country and will advance your financial position as a result. 6, 30

Excrement—There will be many changes in your immediate surroundings. You should be more open in your relationship with others and be ready to express your opinions. 21, 73

Execution—You will suffer setbacks through the carelessness of others. A stay of execution indicates you will overcome all difficulties and achieve happiness and success. 14, 62

Explosion—You will be disappointed in the actions of others. If someone is mutilated or hurt in the explosion, you will be blamed for something you did not do. 43, 61

Eye—Someone is watching you in order to harm you. In love, this dream indicates that someone is trying to take your lover away from you. 31, 81

Eyebrow—You will meet with obstacles in the immediate future. 1, 34

Eyeglasses—You will have disagreeable friends from whom you will have troubles disentangling yourself. 5, 67

—F—

Face—If you see happy faces in a dream, you will have good news and happiness through loved ones. If faces are sad or ugly, beware of lovers' quarrels and forthcoming troubles. 55, 78

Fainting—Illness in the family and sad news. It also indicates you should watch over your health and improve your way of living. 2, 76

Fairy—A favorable omen prognosticating joys and happy times to come. 55, 9

Fall—To dream of falling indicates struggles that will culminate in eventual victories. If you are injured in the fall, you will suffer losses and hardships. 32, 69

Fame—To dream of being famous denotes disappointments in your aspirations. To dream of famous people portends your rise from obscurity to honors and distinctions. 65, 38

Family—A happy family indicates good health and good finances. If there is strife in the family, you will meet with disappointments. 87, 53

Fan—Pleasant news and surprises soon. 51, 3

Farm—To live on one denotes good fortune in all undertakings. 4, 91

Fat—To see yourself fat in a dream denotes fortunate changes. If others are fat, you will have prosperity and good luck. 77, 55

Father—You will meet with difficulties that will require wise counsel from an experienced person. If your father is dead, the dream is a warning against possible business losses. Exercise caution in all your deals. 93, 50

Father-in-law—Quarrels with friends or relatives. If he is well and cheerful in the dream, you will have pleasant family reunions. 73, 46

Fear—Your future will not be as successful as you had hoped for. For a woman this dream predicts a fickle lover and infidelity. 39, 61

Feast—Pleasant surprises are planned for you. 37, 64

Feather—If they fall around you, your burdens in life will be easily borne. Chicken feathers indicate petty annoyances. Black feathers indicate love troubles and sadness in personal matters. 8, 41

Feet—Your own feet predict despair and loss of self-control. To see other people's feet denotes you will be in control of all your affairs and no one will be able to dominate you. 4, 11

Ferns—Your present difficulties will soon be overcome by success and happiness. If the ferns are withered, there will be illness in the family. 13, 50

Ferry—If you cross in one and the water is clear,

you will succeed in all your plans. If the water is murky or turbulent, you will have trouble bringing your plans through to completion. 41, 62

Fever—If you have fever in a dream, you worry over insignificant things and let the best of life pass you by. You should pull yourself together and do more profitable work. 93, 56

Fiance—You will soon experience sad events. 8, 31

Field—To see green fields ripe with fruit denotes abundance in all things. Dry or desolate fields indicate poor prospects. 15, 29

Fight—You will have unpleasant encounters with business and love rivals and possible lawsuits. If you are defeated in a fight, you will lose valuable property. If you win the fight, these bad omens are reversed. 7, 57

Figs—If you eat them, it denotes there is something wrong with your health and you should see a doctor. If you see them growing, it indicates good health and prosperity. 41, 36

Fingernails—If they are well kept, indicates refined tastes and literary achievements. If they are soiled, there will be much unhappiness in your family through erring youths. 81, 32

Fingers—If they are soiled or scratched, you will have much suffering and worries. To see beautiful fingers indicates your love will be requited and you will meet with much happiness. 31, 71

Fire—This is a favorable omen predicting prosperity and a good family life, so long as you do not get burned. If you do, you will suffer losses through impulsive actions. 61, 83

Firearms—Violent and disagreeable arguments that could bring about much grief and sorrow. 49, 6

Fireworks—You will enjoy good health and many pleasures. 27, 31

Fish—If you see them in clear waters, you will be favored by the rich and famous. Dead fish indicate losses through unexpected calamities. To catch fish portends you will enjoy wealth earned through your own merits. 60, 71

Flag—The national flag denotes victory if the country is at war, and prosperity if it is at peace. A foreign flag indicates broken alliances between nations. 72, 14

Fleas—Evil machinations against you. If they bite you, the dream denotes inconstancy in your lover. 8, 21

Flies—The dream denotes sickness and contagious diseases. To women it portends love troubles. 16, 97

Flight—You will make a sudden change that will prove beneficial. 38, 27

Floods—Sickness and loss of business, as well as unhappiness in marriage. 58, 43

Flour—Denotes a simple but harmonious existence. 31, 94

Flower—Pleasure and gain, so long as they are bright and fresh. If they are withered, you will have many disappointments and sadnesses in your life. 88, 25

Flute—If you hear it, you will have a happy reunion with friends who come from a distance. If you play it, you will fall in love with an amiable person. 61, 46

Flying—If you fly high in space, you will have marital difficulties. To fly low indicates sickness and unease which will pass in time. 32, 6

Fog—To travel through a thick fog indicates you will have many business worries. If you come out of it, you will overcome your problems. 20, 36

Food—You will be faced with health problems difficult to diagnose. 66, 31

Forehead—You will change your business or career and will have much success in your new venture. 7, 80

Foreigners—You have lost something of value which you will find when you least expect it. 9, 47

Forest—Loss in trade or business, if you are lost in the forest. If you see a forest green with thick foliage, you will have much happiness and success in all your dealings. 16, 53

Fork—Enemies are working behind your back to cause you troubles. The dream also foretells separations between lovers. 85, 54

Fortress—If you see yourself confined in one, you will be in an unhappy position through the machinations of your enemies. If you see yourself putting others in a fortress, you will overcome your enemies and be very successful with members of the opposite sex. 91, 45

Fountain—If the water in it is clear, you will have vast possessions and many pleasant trips. If the water is cloudy, you will have unhappy love affairs. 61, 32

Fox—To chase one denotes you are involved in shady deals and dangerous love affairs. If you kill one, you will win in all your deals. 54, 37

Freckles—Unpleasant incidents will mar your happiness. 67, 84

Friend—Happiness to come if they are well and happy. If you see them sad or ill, you will have bad news from them. 62, 51

Frog—A noble and wise friend who will always be ready with good advice. 73, 94

Fruit—Ripe fruits in the trees indicate a prosperous future. Green fruits are warnings against hasty actions. To eat fruit is an omen of empty pleasures and possible disappointments through them. 12, 63

Funeral—An unhappy marriage and sickly children. 91, 42

Furniture—Your work will always keep you within the working classes, with very little opportunity of honors or distinction. 32, 76

Furs—To deal in furs denotes prosperity and many varied interests. To be dressed in furs indicates you will never want in life and will always have abundance around you. 99, 7

—G—

Gallows—If you are on one, you will suffer at the hands of malicious people. If a friend suffers this fate, you must be calm in a forthcoming emergency, as you will be able to control the situation. 15, 3

Gambling—If you gamble and win, you will be associated with people of little moral worth. If you lose, your behavior will cause much suffering to someone close to you. 22, 91

Game—Fortunate undertakings and gains through shady business deals. 62, 70

Garage—Your personal affairs will improve in the near future. 16, 32

Garbage—Dangers of scandals and unfavorable business deals. For women this dream foretells love troubles. 58, 14

Garden—If it is filled with flowers and trees, you will have much happiness and peace of mind. Vegetables indicate misery and calumny. But to women this dream foretells fame and happiness. 18, 43

Garlic—You will rise from poverty to prosperity and wealth. To a woman it denotes a marriage of convenience. 22, 36

Gas—If you inhale it, you will have troubles through your own negligence. To extinguish it indicates you will destroy your own happiness. 76, 82

Gasoline—You will have unexpected success from

an unsuspected business source. 39, 12

Gate—To pass through one indicates unhappy news of someone far away. To see a closed gate denotes difficulties in overcoming difficulties. 54, 37

Geranium—You will have considerable wealth in your life. 71, 40

Ghosts—If you see the ghost of one of your parents, you should be careful of business deals with strangers. If the ghost speaks to you, you will be in danger from hidden enemies. 62, 89

Giant—Struggles between you and rivals. If he runs from you, it denotes success and prosperity. 31, 65

Gift—To receive one you will be fortunate in both business and love. 55, 89

Gin—You trust in friends who are not sincere. 78, 44

Girdle—If you wear one, you will be influenced by conniving people. If you receive one, you will enjoy honors and pleasures. 18, 93

Girl—A pleasant, pretty girl indicates happy family life and good business prospects. If she is ungainly or sad, there will be a serious illness in your family. 88, 31

Glass—To look through glass denotes bitter disappointments. To break one or a mirror portends an accidental death. To break glass dishes or windows indicates your business may fail. 79, 65

Gloves—To lose them denotes you will be abandoned by those you love. To wear new gloves indicates you will succeed in your business after some troubles. If they are old, you will be betrayed and suffer losses. 71, 2

Goat—Good weather and a fine harvest. If one attacks you, beware of business competitors. 63, 16

Goblet—You will receive favors from strangers. 66, 51

God—To see God indicates the need to realize your fullest inner potential in order to merge with the Divine within you. The dream tells you it is time to gather your scattered forces and conquer your physical instincts and put them to work for you. 1, 99, 26

Gold—You will be unusually successful in all your enterprises. Your superior talents will make it easy for you to achieve honors and wealth. 15, 72

Golf—Empty daydreams and possible business losses. 83, 54

Gossip—Humiliations and troubles through false friends. 43, 97

Grain—A fortunate omen indicating abundance and prosperity to come. 77, 24

Grandparents—Difficulties which you will overcome by following sound advice from a wise friend or relative. 54, 6

Grapes—Worries and cares, if you eat them. If you see them hanging in the vines, you will soon attain riches and distinctions. 82, 37

—H—

Hair—To comb it means losses in personal affairs through the dreamer's own carelessness. Thinning hair indicates poverty to come through excessive spending. Thick, luxurious hair indicates a life of happiness and prosperity. 9, 55

Hairdresser—Indiscretions in love affairs that may be discovered and which could damage your reputation. 4, 37

Ham—You will be in danger of being used by others. To cut it means you will overpower your rivals and business opponents. To eat it indicates you will lose something of value. 97, 32

Hammer—Difficult obstacles to overcome. 48, 50

Hand—If the hands are beautiful, you will enjoy fame and distinctions. If they are ugly and malformed, denotes poverty and disappointments. If you see your own hands dirty, you will be envious and unfair to others. 35, 67

Handcuffs—If you see yourself handcuffed, you will be in troubles through the machinations of enemies. To see others handcuffed indicates you will be facing an illness and dangers. 79, 42

Handkerchief—Flirtations and inconsequential affairs of the heart. 17, 36

Handwriting—Beware of what you say publicly, as it may be used later on against you by ill-intentioned people. 62, 88

Hanging—Many enemies will get together to overthrow you from your present position. 88, 64

Harlot—You will overindulge in empty pleasures. 58, 94

Harp—To hear it portends the end of a profitable enterprise. To play one means you should be more careful in your choice of friends and lovers. 55, 75

Harvest—Prosperity and pleasures to come, especially if the harvest is abundant. 79, 93

Hash—To eat it means sorrows and vexations are forthcoming. Ill health through worries, as well as petty jealousies and empty pleasures. 11, 8

Hat—A new hat indicates a change of place and of business, which will be advantageous. To lose your hat indicates unsatisfactory business affairs and irresponsible associates. 82, 8

Hate—This dream is an evil omen predicting injuries through spiteful actions. 98, 66

Hawk—You will be cheated by designing persons if you are not careful. To see one dead or to kill one indicates you will overcome your enemies. 8, 43

Hay—To mow it denotes a good life and great prosperity. To see it portends good fortune and success in all your dealings. 7, 14

Head—If you see your own head, you will face nervous troubles. If you see other people's heads and they are well-formed and attractive, you will meet prominent and important people who may be of much help to you. A severed head denotes bitter disappointments in life. 87, 35

Hearse—Quarrels at home and failures in business. If it crosses your path, you will be faced with a dangerous enemy. 13, 46

Heart—If your heart pains and troubles you, there will be losses in your business affairs. To see it indicates sickness and lack of energy. 68, 52

Heat—Failure to carry out your plans as you expected. 51, 18

Heaven—If you ascend to heaven in a dream, you will see your joys transformed into sadness. For a young person to climb on a ladder, they will reach a prominent position in life. 13, 10

Heir—You may lose your possessions and will gain new responsibilities. 75, 47

Hell—To be in hell indicates you will be tempted to do something that may endanger your finances and your mental peace. To see your friends in hell indicates you may hear of their misfortunes. 88, 38

Hen—Happy family reunions and good times. 55, 3

Herbs—You will be receiving much love. 12, 7

Hermit—Sadness and loneliness may soon cross your path through the unfaithfulness of friends. 6, 17

High school—High positions in social and business affairs and good fortune in love. 55, 19

Hill—To climb one indicates honor and distinctions to come. To fall from one means you will have to contend with much envy and jealousy. 48, 60

Hips—Well-formed hips denote you will have marital or love difficulties. Narrow hips predict sickness and disappointments. 13, 4

Hogs—Fortunate business changes and success in personal affairs if hogs are fat and healthy. If they are thin and dirty, predicts difficulties and worries. 74, 38

Hole—You will soon be facing a long journey. 91, 23

Home—To visit your old home portends you will rejoice over good news. If it is in a run-down condition, you will soon hear of the sickness or death of a relative. 88, 42

Honey—You will be in the possession of great wealth. To eat it indicates you will enjoy both wealth and love. 55, 7

Hood—To wear it means you will behave in an unbecoming manner. 8, 69

Hook—You will be faced with disagreeable obligations. 3, 28

Horn—If you hear one, you will receive news soon that will fill you with great happiness. If you blow one, you are more anxious to marry than your lover. 7, 78

Hornet—Breakups between old friends and money losses. 94, 13

Horoscope—To dream of having it prepared indicates unexpected changes and a long journey. 27, 89

Horse—Rise in fortune and gratification of your desires, if you ride a healthy, beautiful horse. To see them denotes success and high living, as well as a great passion in your life. 15, 90

Horseshoe—Business gains and love affairs that

turn into marriage. To pick one up indicates you will have profits from an unknown source. 16, 35

Hospital—There is the danger of contagious diseases in your vicinity. 27, 72

Hotel—You will travel extensively and enjoy much success and happiness in your life. 52, 34

House—A new house indicates a change of residence and happy business deals. If the house is old and dilapidated, you will have business losses and poor health. 65, 38

Howl—You can expect bad news soon. 78, 20

Hunchback—Unexpected changes for the worse in your affairs. 8, 13

Hunger—An unfortunate omen indicating an unhappy marriage and troubles at home. 22, 6

Hunt—You will struggle to attain the impossible, unless you find and catch your game. In this case, you will meet with joys. 1, 90

Hurricane—You will encounter much suffering and difficulties in your immediate future. Be strong and you will overcome. 8, 1

Husband—Many changes in your life. If you see him dead, you will meet with many disappointments and sorrows. If he is healthy and happy, your home will be filled with much joy and pleasures. 55, 7

Hut—Ill health and dissatisfaction in your affairs. 87, 14

Hydrophobia—Beware of enemies and rivals who will try to cause you grief and losses. 17, 46

Hyena—Bad luck and disappointments. Also lovers' quarrels indicated. 15, 64

Hysteria—Try to remain in control in an upcoming difficult situation as you will overcome it. 98, 76

—I—

Ice—Much distress and danger through enemies and opponents. If you see ice floating on clear water, you will suffer through jealous and impatient friends. To walk on ice is a warning not to take unnecessary risks. 80, 49

Ice cream—To eat it foretells you will meet with much success in your affairs. If it melts, your hopes will not be realized. 24, 35

Icicles—Sadness and misfortune will soon vanish from your life. 16, 63

Idol—Slow progress on your way to the top. 56, 43

Illness—Be careful not to make an erroneous decision at this time. 17, 39

Imp—Beware of empty pleasures tempting you into destroying your life. 78

Incense—Do not let others flatter you into doing their will. 88, 78

Incest—Losses in business and in public opinion. 73, 26

Indifference—Pleasant companions who will not

be with you for very long. 38, 94

Indigestion—You must try to improve your eating habits and your surroundings. 23, 47

Injury—An unhappy event will soon cause you grief. Try to be strong about it, as it will pass. 11, 57

Ink—To spill it indicates suffering through the envy of others. To see it indicates dangerous rivals and unsuccessful business deals. 18, 77

Insanity—Ill health and disagreeable changes are near. Watch your health and eating habits. 66, 46

Inundation—Misfortunes and loss of life through unforeseeable catastrophes. 18, 69

Invalid—Disagreeable companions and troubles in your affairs. 11, 2

Invisible—You may make a costly error if you are not careful. 77, 54

Invitation—Unpleasant events and worries over trifles. 64, 30

Iron—An omen of distress and unfortunate circumstances. 28, 50

Ironing—Domestic comforts and a happy family life. If you burn your hands, you will have to contend with jealousy and a possible illness. 21, 76

Island—If it is pleasant and green, you will enjoy many comforts and success in all your dealings. If it is barren, you may suffer emotional and material losses through intemperance. 28, 67

Itch—You tend to worry over trifles. Relax and all will be well. 67, 57

Ivory—Good fortune and financial success. 90, 42

Ivy—You will enjoy excellent health and increase in good fortune and happy love affairs. 55, 7

—J—

Jade—You will soon have prosperity and happiness. 7, 67

Jail—You will be asked to grant privileges to people you consider unworthy of them. Use your better judgment. 26, 56

Jam—To eat it denotes pleasant surprises and happy journeys. 10, 5

Jar—If the jar is empty, you will meet poverty and distress. If it is full, you will have success in your work. 36, 71

Jaws—Disagreements and ill feelings between friends. Also there is a possibility of illness for you or someone close to you. 1, 63

Jealousy—Worries and quarrels among lovers or between husband and wife. Also beware of enemies' influence around you. 23, 90

Jelly—Pleasant reunions with friends. 76, 54

Jewelry—Pleasure and riches will be yours. To wear them denotes you will reach a high position in life. 77, 68

Jockey—You will receive a gift from an unexpected source. 98, 53

Joke—You should try to enjoy your life as long as you can. 71, 60

Joker—If you are interested in marriage, you will soon have the opportunity to take that step. 8, 91

Journey—Profit if the trip is pleasant and losses if the trip is disagreeable. 65, 32

Judge—Disputes will be settled through legal proceedings. 43, 2

Judgment Day—You will accomplish something you have carefully planned for a long time. 99, 6

Jug—You have many good friends who will get together to help you in times of trouble. 2, 13

Juggler—Beware of extravagant spending. 41, 70

Jumping—If you dream of jumping over something, you will succeed in overcoming all obstacles. If you fall in the jump, you may soon be faced with love troubles and business losses. 42, 89

Jungle—You will face strong business opponents and difficulties in all public relations. 32, 64

Jury—If you are a member of the jury, you are dissatisfied with your present line of work and will try to change your trade or profession. If you are cleared through a jury, you will succeed in all your affairs. If you are condemned, your enemies will overcome you. 88, 48

Justice—Watch your actions and public behavior, for you may soon be faced with scandals and social embarrassments. 13, 47

—K—

Kaleidoscope—Swift changes with little promise for betterment. 4, 32

Kangaroo—To see one indicates you will overcome an enemy who seeks to destroy you. 43, 28

Keg—You will be faced with misfortunes and a possible separation from your family. 9, 57

Kettle—Much hard work lies ahead. If the kettle is filled with boiling water, your struggles will soon end in victory. 6, 81

Key—Unexpected changes in your life. To find keys indicates you will have a happy domestic life and good business proposals. To lose a key portends disagreeable adventures and experiences. 11, 29

Keyhole—This dream portends jealousy and quarrels. 8, 43

Kick—You will soon solve your present problems. 3, 65

Kid—Beware of light pleasures and flirtations, or you will hurt someone who loves you very much. 58, 62

Kidneys—You may be threatened with a serious illness. Also there is the possibility of marital strife or lovers' quarrels around you. 15, 8

Killing—Sorrow and failure in all your affairs, if you do the killing. But if you kill in self-defense, the dream denotes victory and business improvements. 4, 49

King—Your ambitions can get the best of you if they are not controlled or directed along more constructive lines. 12, 73

Kiss—If you kiss somebody in a dream, you will have honors and riches and will be much loved by friends and family. 4, 21

Kitchen—You will be faced with emergencies and disagreeable events. 14, 72

Kite—To fly a kite denotes you will show off in front of friends, without any basis or reason. If the kite falls to the ground, you will have disappointments in business. 6, 38

Kitten—Beware of deceptions. You will have many small troubles that will vex and annoy you. 36. 47

Knapsack—You will find the greatest and happiest surprises among total strangers. 39, 27

Knee—This is an unfortunate omen that forbodes troubles and bad luck. 17, 62

Knife—This dream portends quarrels and separations as well as business losses. 98, 56

Knitting—Peace and quiet in the home with a loving companion and pleasant children. If a woman dreams of knitting, she will soon get married if she is single. 77, 5

Knocking—Serious news is forthcoming. 36, 42

Knot—You will worry over trifles. To tie knots signifies you have an independent nature and will not allow yourself to be controlled by your lover or spouse. 16, 40

Knuckle—You love someone who does not love you in return. 23, 95

—L—

Label—Do not let an enemy learn anything about your private affairs or he or she will use what he/she learns to harm you. 13, 8

Labor—Profitable work and excellent health. 65, 74

Laboratory—You may be faced with a serious illness if you do not watch over your health. 47, 35

Lace—You will have difficulties with an enemy who poses as a friend. 14, 24

Ladder—Your hopes will be realized, only if you climb one. 57, 78

Lagoon—Doubts and confusion through hasty decisions. 43, 27

Lake—If you sail on a smooth lake, you will have happiness and satisfactions which you will share with loved ones. If the waters are muddy or turbulent, the dream predicts problems in love and business. 33, 89

Lamb—Happy friendships and simple joys. If the lamb is dead or is slaughtered, you will meet with unhappiness and many losses. 75, 36

Lame—Your wishes will not be realized. 25, 97

Lament—Struggles and distress which will give way to eventual happiness and success. 24, 86

Lamp—Joys and many pleasures if the lamp is lighted. Dark or empty lamps denote depression and sadness. 32, 10

Lance—You will face powerful enemies that could cause you many difficulties. 16, 53

Landscape—You will achieve many honors and distinctions. 17, 61

Lantern—To see one shining ahead of you in the darkness, you will possess wealth and position. If it goes out, you will fail to achieve your ambitions. 24, 56

Lap—If you sit on someone's lap, you will be free from cares and problems. If someone sits on your lap, you will be faced with unfavorable criticism. 68, 79

Laugh—Success in all your undertakings, and many pleasant companions. Mocking laughter indicates you will face illness and disappointments. 76, 54

Laundry—If the clothes are clean, your enterprises will meet with success. If they are dirty, you will meet with failure. It is a bad omen if the laundryman comes to your house to pick up the laundry. If he does, you may soon face an illness or lose something of great value. 13, 67

Laurel—Success and fame will someday be yours. Gains in all your enterprises. 75, 48

Lawn—You will have prosperity in all your affairs. 12, 56

Lawsuit—Beware, as enemies are trying to destroy your public image. 29, 90

Lawyer—Be careful not to commit indiscretions which may prove costly in the long run. 43, 28

Lead—Disappointments in business and personal affairs. Expect also troubles in love. 58, 49

Leak—Losses and tribulations. 98, 76

Leaping—You will gain your wishes after a great deal of struggle. 79, 32

Leather—Success in business and in love. Favorable speculations and much fortune and happiness in all aspects of your life. 55, 9

Leaves—Happiness and satisfaction in your business deals. Dry leaves denote false hopes and forthcoming disappointments. 78, 17

Ledger—Confusion and doubts if you keep one. To make the wrong entries into a ledger indicates small disputes and a slight loss. If ledger is destroyed by fire, you will suffer losses through the carelessness of friends. 17, 23

Leeches—Enemies are trying to overcome you in business. 21, 45

Legislature—Vanity and selfishness are predicted by this dream. You will find difficulties in advancing in your general affairs. 13, 64

Legs—Clean and shapely legs indicate happy ventures and good friends. If legs are amputated or cannot be used, you will meet disappointments and poverty. 22, 34

Lemon—Jealousy and possible disappointments and humiliations, especially if you eat the lemon. 81, 73

Lemonade—Someone will try to make money at your expense. 14, 67

Lending—You will have troubles meeting your obligations. 42, 95

Leopard—If it attacks you, misplaced confidence can shatter your fondest dreams. If you kill one, you will triumph in all your affairs. If you see one caged, your enemies will not be able to hurt you. 87, 56

Leprosy—If you see yourself infected with this disease, you will soon face an expensive illness. If others suffer from it, it denotes discouraging prospects and love troubles. 11, 19

Letter—If you dream of getting a pleasant letter, you will meet with much happiness soon. If you get unpleasant news, you will have troubles and possibly an illness to contend with. 72, 34

Lettuce—If the lettuce is green and clean, you are about to have an embarrassment that will be followed by the achievement of one of your fondest wishes. If you eat it, you will suffer from jealous pangs and perhaps from an illness that may separate you from your lover. 15, 64

Liar—Vexations through deceitful people. 15, 48

Library—To find yourself in one indicates you will be disappointed and discontented in your environment and will seek special studies to bring new interests into your life. 24, 3

Lice—Worries and distress, as well as the possibility of a serious ailment. 22, 31

License—Quarrels and losses are possible. 12, 34

Lifeboat—You will escape from a threatened evil. If it sinks, your own friends will cause you much distress. 56, 78

Light—Success in all your dealings. Dim light indicates partial success. If the light goes out, you will meet with disappointment in a much-planned enterprise. 34, 56

Lighthouse—If you see one in the middle of a calm sea, you will have many joys and pleasant friends. If you see the lighthouse through a storm, your sorrows will eventually be replaced by prosperity and happiness. 34, 87

Lightning—Happiness and prosperity, but of short duration. If it strikes you, unexpected sorrows will befall you in love and business both. 66, 47

Lilac—Beware of vanity and conceit, for they could be your downfall. 14, 45

Lily—You will suffer much grief through illness and death, if you see a lily. But if they are growing in large quantities on a green field, the dream denotes early marriage followed by widowhood. 6, 68

Linen—Prosperity and happiness. 32, 73

Lion—You have much inner strength and great dignity which will always help you succeed in life. If the lion overpowers you, you will be at the mercy of your enemies. 13, 85

Lips—Soft, full lips indicate harmony and power. In love they predict reciprocation of your affection. Thin lips denote mastery of every situation. 27, 82

Liquor—To buy it indicates you will appropriate something that is not yours. To drink it denotes possible acquisition of wealth, which you will generously share with others. To see it denotes success and prosperity. 85, 42

Liver—A sick liver denotes you will have a spouse who will never cease to complain about life in general. If you eat liver in a dream, you will learn that a deceitful person has taken your place in your lover's affections. 8, 87

Lizard—Attacks from enemies. Misfortune and sorrows if it bites or strikes you. 28, 92

Loaf—This dream indicates frugality. If they multiply, you will meet with success. 22, 43

Lobster—Great favors from important people and many riches. 63, 37

Lock—Confusion and doubt. In love, it means you will find the means to overcome a rival. If you cannot open it, you will suffer severe losses and sorrows. 91, 65

Locomotive—A rapid advancement in your career and many pleasant travels. If it is broken or derailed you will suffer severe losses and sorrows. 91,65

Locusts—Discrepancies in your business which will cause you many worries. 74, 56

Log—You will be surrounded by abundance and joy. 55, 19

Lord's Prayer—You are in danger through enemies and will need the help of friends to save you from this threat. 23, 46

Lottery—If you win it, you will gain in a doubtful business in which you are now engaged. If you lose, you will be the victim of deceitful people. If others win, you will enjoy many happy reunions with good friends. 63, 32

Love—Satisfaction with your environment. Success in your affairs and freedom from anxiety. 75, 69

Lucky—You may expect the fulfillment of your wishes. 6, 14

Luggage—Unpleasant duties and obligations. If you carry it, you will have great sorrows and troubles in life. 27, 49

Lung—You may be facing a serious illness. 59, 83

Lying—Dishonorable actions and unjust criticism will be suffered by you or inflicted by you on others. 18, 77

—M—

Macaroni—Small losses. For a woman the dream means that a stranger will soon enter her life. 18, 70

Machinery—A new enterprise will fill you with great anxiety, but will eventually culminate in success. 29, 57

Madness—You may expect troubles and difficulties in the near future. 34, 42

Magazine—You will receive news from a distance. 31, 76

Magic—If you accomplish something by means of magic in a dream, you will have pleasant surprises. If you see a magician in a dream, you will enjoy many interesting travels. 54, 17

Magnet—Beware of evil influences that will attempt to tempt you into mischief. For a woman the dream foretells someone will shower gifts and much wealth upon her. 46, 84

Mail—Very good news is forthcoming. 87, 67

Make-up—Someone may be trying to deceive you. 85, 71

Malice—You must try to control your passions. 32, 45

Man—A good-looking man in a dream indicates you will enjoy a full and happy life. If the man is ugly or misshapen, you will meet with many disappointments. 23, 45

Mansion—Wealthy possessions will be yours. If the mansion is haunted, you will meet with sudden misfortunes in the midst of happiness. 48, 71

Manuscript—If it is unfinished, it foretells disappointments. If it is well-written and finished, you will realize your greatest hopes. 32, 91

Map—Changes in your business which will bring about some disappointments, but also much peril. 56, 82

Marble—You will meet with much success financially, but your social life will be empty of affection. 15, 41

Marijuana—Unrealizable hopes will haunt your dreams. You must try to deal more comfortably with reality. 16, 3

Market—Thrift and much activity in your occupation. If the market is empty, it denotes depression and sadness. 12, 82

Marriage—To see one denotes much pleasure in the future. If you see yourself getting married, you will receive disagreeable news from someone far away. 67, 16

Mars—You will suffer much unhappiness through the cruelty of certain so-called friends. Also beware of enemies trying to harm you. 18, 51

Martyr—You will gain many honors and distinctions. 73, 91

Mask—If you wear one, you will be faced with temporary problems. To see others wearing masks denotes you will have to deal with falsehoood and envy. 41, 58

Mat—You will be faced with sorrow and many worries. 21, 70

Matches—Prosperity and changes when you least expect them. 54, 39

Mattress—New duties and responsibilities will soon be faced by you. 63, 27

Mausoleum—Sickness, death or sorrows to a famous friend. If you find yourself inside the mausoleum, you will be faced with your own sickness. 13, 85

Measles—Many worries and anxieties over your business affairs if you have the measles. If someone else has the disease, you will be concerned over this person. 62, 9

Meat—Raw meat indicates much worry and discouragement in your career. Cooked meat signifies that others will achieve that which you desire. 5, 19

Mechanic—Changes of residence and a more active business. 92, 4

Medal—Honors acquired through hard work and devotion. To lose a medal indicates sadness and difficulties through the unfaithfulness of others. 33, 8

Medicine—If the medicine is pleasant to the taste, you will meet with troubles, but you will find a solution that will be to your best advantage. If the medicine is unpleasant, you will face an illness or a loss. If you administer the medicine to others, you will hurt someone who trusts in you. 77, 25

Melon—The friend you trust the most laughs at you behind your back. 47, 38

Mermaid—You will suffer disappointments in your love life. 32, 44

Message—Changes in your affairs, if you receive one. If you send one, you will find yourself in unpleasant situations. 16, 5

Mice—Domestic troubles and insincere friends. Also a bad omen for business. 77, 1

Microscope—Failure and small gains in your business. 9, 12

Milk—To drink it indicates abundance and pleasure. To see it in large quantities portends riches and vibrant health. To spill it means you will suffer some loss and temporary unhappiness at the hands of friends. 6, 14

Millionaire—You should listen to friends' advice. 10, 2

Mine—Failure in your affairs. To own one denotes future riches. 23, 60

Minister—Misfortunes and unpleasant changes and journeys. 38, 50

Mirror—To see yourself in one denotes distress and illness. To see others means they will use you for their own interests. A broken mirror indicates the sudden or violent death of someone close to you. 8, 13

Miscarriage—Many joys and happiness to come. 17, 7

Miser—Unhappiness and sorrows through your own selfishness. 10, 32

Mist—Uncertain future and unhappiness at home. 5, 61

Mistletoe—Happiness and great rejoicing. 44, 6

Money—Small worries followed by much happiness. Many changes for the best in your life, unless it leaves your hands; in that case, losses. 82, 46

Monk—Family troubles and unpleasant journeys. 15, 80

Monkey—Betrayal and deceit are imminent. 18, 66

Monster—If he pursues you, you will meet with sorrows and worries soon. To kill one denotes you will overcome your enemies and rise to a high position. 1, 22

Moon—Changes for the best in business, and success in love affairs. 65, 34

Mother—A happy reunion with a loved one. 2, 85

Mother-in-law—Pleasant reconciliations with someone you love. 11, 70

Mountain—To climb one indicates rise to wealth and distinctions. If you fall off one or cannot reach the top, you will meet with reverses and disappointments. 8, 60

Mud—Losses and troubles in the family. Beware of false friends. 64, 42

Murder—Much sorrow through the misdeeds of others. A bad omen that foretells deceit, dishonor and general misfortune. 88, 94

Museum—You will acquire many valuables along your life. 3, 57

Mushroom—To see one indicates greed and unspeakable desires. To eat one denotes humiliations and shameful love affairs. 78, 69

Music—Pleasure and prosperity. 24, 63

Mustache—To wear one indicates selfishness and betrayal. 71, 2

Mute—Trials in life and misfortunes. 66, 18

Mystery—Changes for the best in your life. Beware of neglecting your duties. 26, 4

—N—

Nails—Much work for little gain. If they are rusty, beware of illness and business losses. 64, 82

Naked—If you are naked in a dream, you will face scandals and unwise engagements. If others are naked, you will be tempted to abandon your duties. Beware of deceitful friends. 88, 54

Napkin—Happy reunions. 34, 55

Narcotics—Faithfulness to your duties to others. 3, 25

Navel—Beware of sudden unpleasant news concerning your parents. 15, 68

Navy—Victorious struggles and control of enemies. Many happy journeys are indicated. 99, 57

Neck—Broken relationships and separations. 24, 5

Necklace—A beautiful home and loving spouse. 11, 87

Needle—Worries and misfortunes to come. 71, 44

Neighbor—Useless gossip and struggles, and the possibility of quarrels. 46, 15

Nephew—You will soon enjoy gains in business. 79, 51

Nest—A new enterprise will prove lucky. To a woman it foretells a change in residence. 19, 43

Net—Troubles and deceit. 18, 32

News—Good news portends fortunate affairs. Bad news indicates the contrary. 71, 28

Newspaper—Beware of fraud in your dealings, for you may be discovered. 88, 78

New Year—Unexpected prosperity and happy marriage. 77, 10

Niece—Trials and useless worry in the near future. 94, 62

Night—Unusual oppressions and hardships in business. 16, 39

Nightmare—Failure in business. Watch what you eat. 21, 98

Noodles—Abnormal appetite and desires. A bad omen. 44, 90

Nose—Changes in your business affairs, usually for the best. 67, 27

Numbers—Unsettled conditions in business will cause you many dissatisfactions. 14, 73

Nun—Possible separation between lovers. 92, 36

Nurse—You will need others' help in order to solve a pressing problem. 74, 56

Nut—Successful enterprises and happy love affairs. 55, 7

Nymph—Passionate desires will be realized. 35, 97

—O—

Oak—Great prosperity in all aspects of life. 32, 94

Oasis—Pleasant reunion with an old, dear friend. 56, 42

Oath—Dissensions and troubles soon. 15, 8

Oatmeal—To eat it denotes the enjoyment of well-earned fortune. 65, 39

Obituary—Bad news soon. 8, 16

Ocean—If it appears calm, you will enjoy profitable business deals. If the ocean appears turbulent, it foretells your narrow escape from injury and the designs of enemies. 15, 76

Oculist—You will be unhappy with your progress in life. 17, 54

Office—You may soon face a contender for the affections of your lover. 32, 91

Oil—You will be controlling your destiny and the destinies of others. Large quantities of oil indicate pleasure excesses. 14, 82

Old Man—Unhappy cares and disagreeable duties will disturb you. 13, 73

Old Woman—Many sorrows in the near future. 23, 78

Olives—Successful business deals and happy surprises. To eat them indicates contentment and faithful friends. 45, 62

Omelet—Beware of flattery and deceit. If you eat it, someone you trust will abuse your friendship. 34, 61

Omnibus—Misunderstandings with friends and false promises. 81, 47

Onion—Envy and spite around you because of some success you will have. To eat it denotes triumphs in all your endeavors. 31, 67

Opera—You will be entertained by congenial friends, and all your affairs will work out favorably for some time to come. 74, 39

Opium—Strangers will bring you difficulties in business. 86, 50

Oranges—To see healthy orange trees loaded with fruit indicates good health and prosperity. To eat oranges indicates sicknesses of friends or relatives, as well as dissatisfaction in your business. 7, 55

Orangutang—Someone is using your influence to advance their own selfish schemes. Deceit between lovers is also indicated. 11, 83

Orchard—To see a rich orchard, laden with fruit, indicates you will receive recognition for work well done and will enjoy a happy home life. If the orchard is barren, you will miss the opportunity to rise to a higher position in life. 59, 62

Orchestra—To hear one denotes you will be well liked because of your kindness to others. If you see yourself playing in an orchestra, you will have pleasant pastimes and enjoy the love of your spouse or lover. 4, 92

Organ—To hear one indicates lasting friendships and a growing fortune. To see one in a church indicates death in families or separations. 14, 87

Orphan—You will benefit from the work of others. 33, 75

Ostrich—You will build up a great fortune in secret. Also you may engage in illicit intrigues with women. 63, 28

Oven—If the oven is red hot, you will have the love of your family and a large number of children. If you bake in the oven, you will meet with temporary disappointments. 62, 40

Overcoat—Unfortunate experiences through the mistakes of strangers, if you borrow one. To wear or see a good-looking one means your wishes will be realized. 57, 28

Owl—To hear the screech of an owl denotes death is near. Bad news from someone far away is also possible. To see one indicates danger from enemies. 96, 74

Ox—You will become a leader in your community. Also there is the possibility of marriage in the near future, if the ox is yoked and matched with another. 55, 37

Oyster—To see oysters denotes easy living and many children to come. If you eat them, you will engage in low pleasures. 46, 15

—P—

Package—To receive one indicates pleasant recreations. To send one means you will experience minor losses. 81, 7

Page—Beware of breaking the law. 65, 4

Pagoda—To see one denotes you will soon be able to go on a long-planned journey. To be in one with a lover means many unexpected events will happen before you get married. 90, 31

Pail—An enpty pail indicates famine or poor crops. A pail full of milk indicates good prospects and fine friends. 65, 29

Pain—To be in pain indicates useless worries over trivial things. To see others in pain means you are making mistakes in your life. 78, 16

Paint—To have paint on your clothes denotes unhappiness through the thoughtlessness of others. To see newly painted houses indicates you will succeed with some devised plans. 33, 46

Painting—To see beautiful paintings warns of deceitful friends and of elusive pleasures. If you see yourself painting, you are satisfied with your present work. 56, 92

Palace—Profits and distinctions. 55, 38

Pallbearer—You will cause trouble for yourself by antagonizing important people, as well as friends. 73, 24

Palmistry—You will be the object of suspicion. 82, 69

Palm Tree—You will improve your situation in life and will find much happiness in love. If the palms are withered, the omen is reversed. 8, 61

Pancake—Great success in all enterprises. 4, 83

Panther—To see one indicates losses in business. If you kill or overpower it, you will meet with great success. 18, 3

Paper—Losses through lawsuits and quarrels at home. 73, 51

Parachute—You will suffer losses through your own excesses. 13, 6

Parade—You may be sure of the love and faithfulness of your lover. 55, 14

Paradise—You have loyal friends who want to help you. If you are sick and poor, this dream predicts a quick recovery and an improvement in your financial situation. 35, 42

Paralysis—You will probably have to face financial reverses and disappointments in literary hopes. Also troubles in love. 17, 36

Parcel—To receive one denotes you will be pleasantly surprised by the return of an absent person whom you love. To carry one means you will have to perform an unpleasant task. 27, 81

Pardon—Your present difficulties will be resolved advantageously for you. 56, 73

Parents—If they seem well and happy, you may expect pleasant changes in your life. If they appear in your dreams after they have died, it is a warning of coming trouble. 43, 85

Park—Pleasant parks denotes happy leisure hours. Ill-kept parks predict unexpected bad turns. 97, 48

Parrot—If they chatter, it signifies you waste your time in idle talk and unimportant things. 65, 72

Parsley—Hard-earned triumphs at work, good health and a happy home life. If you eat it, you can expect good health but a lot of hard work supporting your family. 66, 53

Parting—To part with those close to you predicts you will be facing many annoying trifles soon. If you part with enemies, your love and business life will improve. 29, 78

Partner—If your partner is a man, you will have uncertainty and ups and downs in money matters. A woman partner indicates secret business deals. 67, 53

Party—You will be faced with monetary problems. 87, 20

Passenger—Improvements in your daily life if they arrive. If they leave, you will lose the opportunity of acquiring a much-desired piece of property. 33, 89

Pastry—To see it denotes deceit and treachery. To eat it means you have good, faithful friends. 18, 57

Patch—If you wear patches on your clothes you are not ashamed to fulfill all your obligations, no matter how painful they may seem. If others wear patches, poverty may be near. 8, 67

Path—To dream you are walking a narrow or rocky path indicates you will soon have a bout with adversity. If the path is covered or bordered with flowers, you will soon be free from an oppressive lover. 99, 5

Pawnshop—To enter one indicates losses and disappointments. To redeem a pledge means you will regain a lost position. 76, 22

Peach—Happiness and success in all your dealings. 34, 82

Peacock—You will be deceived in a lover's sense of honor. Beware of deceptive appearances. 88, 47

Pear—To eat them denotes bad health and lack of success. To see them in the tree is a good omen predicting an improvement in your affairs. 6, 93

Pearl—Your business will improve and you will have a pleasant surprise soon. 11, 74

Peas—Good health and the accumulation of wealth. 65, 40

Pebbles—You will be faced with many rivals that threaten your peace of mind. 17, 64

Pen—You may be led into troubles by your love of adventure. 24, 9

Pencil—Favorable occupations that bring good remunerations. 62, 2

Penitentiary—Unhappiness at home and failure in your business. 29, 78

Penny—Unsatisfactory business deals and troubles in love. If you find them, improvements in your affairs. 12, 6

Pepper—Many worries and troubles through your love of gossip. Beware of deceit around you. 23, 42

Peppermint—Many pleasures and enjoyable affairs. 35, 59

Perfume—To smell it indicates happy events will take place in your life. To spill it means you will lose something you like very much. 82, 4

Perspiration—Present troubles will soon dissipate and be replaced with honors. 19, 3

Pest—Disagreeable event will soon take place in your life. 83, 61

Photography—Beware of deception and dissension around you. 27, 83

Physician—You waste your time in frivolous pastimes. 61, 85

Piano—To see one indicates a happy event to come. To play one means you will succeed in conquering a potential lover. To hear piano music predicts good health and success in all things. 24, 7

Pickles—You are wasting your energies in a luckless pursuit. 13, 8

Pickpocket—Someone will harass and trouble you, causing you losses. 28, 16

Picnic—Happiness to come and much success. 19, 1

Pictures—Beware of deceit and the ill will of those around you. 18, 77

Pig—A healthy, fat pig is an indication of fair success in business. 38, 64

Pigeon—To see or hear pigeons denotes domestic peace and pleasant children. 17, 5

Pill—Many responsibilities with little rewards. 8, 16

Pillow—Luxury and comfort. 73, 9

Pimple—If you see your face covered with them, you will be bothered by many trifles. 14, 27

Pineapple—If you gather or eat them, you will meet with much success in the near future. 67, 3

Pine Tree—Much success in all your affairs. 17, 46

Pins—Quarrels and dissension at home. To be pricked by one means someone will irritate you. 21, 74

Pipe—Sewer, gas or any other type of pipe portends much prosperity in your community. To smoke a pipe means you will be visited by an old friend. 14, 36

Pirate—You will be in danger through the deceptions of false friends. If you are a pirate in a dream, you will lose the support and esteem of former friends and associates. 24, 75

Pistol—To see one portends bad luck to come. To shoot one, beware of jumping to the wrong conclusion and being unfair to someone as a result. 26, 14

Pit—To look into a deep pit indicates you will take unnecessary risks in business and be indiscreet in your love affairs. If you fall into the pit, it denotes calamities and sorrows to come. 27, 16

Pitcher—Success in your business. 32, 14

Plague—Many disappointments in store for you, including troubles with your spouse or lover. 57, 13

Plain—To cross one indicates you will have luck in finding a wonderful position, providing the plain is covered with grass. If it is dry and arid, the opposite will come to pass. 18, 53

Planet—A disagreeable journey and depressing work are in store for you. 26, 32

Plate—To a woman this dream indicates a good husband and a happy home life. 37, 67

Play—You will realize your fondest hopes. 23, 74

Pleasure—Many gains and personal enjoyments. 73, 96

Plow—Unusual success in all your affairs. 32, 75

Plums—Ripe plums denote happy events will come into your life soon. If you gather them, you will obtain your desires but they will prove evanescent. 78, 14

Pocket—Evil designs planned against you. 67, 83

Pocketbook—To lose it indicates disagreements with a close friend. To find one full of money indicates good luck and the achievement of your heart's desire. 48, 27

Poison—Unpleasantness and difficulties around you. 62, 43

Poker—To play it indicates you should beware against evil people. 83, 14

Police—You will succeed in overcoming rivals, so long as the police do not arrest you. If they do, beware of danger around you. 76, 82

Politician—Misunderstandings and ill feelings between you and your associates and close family. 54, 89

Polka—To dance it indicates pleasant occupations. 76, 43

Pony—Moderate speculations will meet with success. 68, 91

Poor—Worries and losses. 15, 39

Pope—You will bow to some master if the Pope does not speak. If he speaks to you, you will attain high honors and distinctions. 34, 83

Postage—Good organization in your business which will prove very rewarding financially. 57, 62

Postman—Disagreeable news could be forthcoming. 33, 7

Potatoes—Success and substantial gains in business. 37, 51

Powder—Beware of deceitful people around you. 41, 98

Prayer—You will be in danger of failures in your affairs. 11, 23

Preacher—Your affairs will not march as they should. Beware of errors of judgment. 41, 60

Pregnancy—If a woman sees herself pregnant, she will be unhappy in her married life. If she happens to be pregnant in real life, this dream predicts a safe and happy delivery. 26, 1

Priest—An omen of misfortunes to come. 78, 45

Prince—A present will be received by you. 67, 93

Princess—Beware of pride and arrogance, especially with your friends. 34, 67

Printer—You must practice economy or you will be faced with poverty. 24, 18

Prison—An evil omen, predicting misfortunes and unhappiness, unless you see someone leaving it. 44, 6

Prize—Have faith in yourself, for you will overcome all difficulties. 22, 16

Prostitute—Your honesty and good will may soon be doubted. 4, 27

Prunes—You will face many difficulties in your life. 90, 16

Pudding—Disappointments and poor success in your affairs. 18, 54

Puddle—Disturbing events that will turn out for the best in the long run. 25, 43

Pulpit—You will meet with disappointments in business and sorrows in your life. 29, 63

Pump—Much energy that will result in business success. 38, 44

Pumpkin—You will witness the dishonor of a friend. 87, 47

Pup—You will show kindness to those in need and enjoy much happiness as a result. 61, 53

Purse—A purse filled with money or jewels indicates much joy, harmony and love will be yours. 73, 29

Pyramid—Many changes in store for you. If you climb one, you will go a long way before reaching your goal in life. 61, 36

—Q—

Quack—You will worry over the proper treatment of an illness. 17, 45

Quail—Disagreeable news is forthcoming. 14, 78

Quarantine—You will be in a bad position due to the evil designs of enemies. 82, 48

Quarrel—Much unhappiness and arguments around you. 13, 62

Quarry—If men are at work in the quarry, you will advance in life through hard work. If the quarry is empty, you will meet disappointments and sorrows. 17, 69

Quarter—Unfortunate business affairs. 24, 50

Queen—Successful ventures. 77, 16

Question—You will be honest in your deals and successful in your business. 32, 81

Quicksand—You will meet with deceitful people and suffer losses as a result. 28, 73

Quilt—You will find your future protected through comfortable circumstances. 16, 48

Quiver—Your love life will improve in the very near future. 32, 51

—R—

Rabbi—Favorable changes around you. 17, 56

Rabbit—Business gains and happiness in love and in family life, if married. 77, 3

Raccoon—You are being deceived by enemies posing as friends. 18, 93

Race—Others want the things you want. If you win the race, they will not get them and you will. If you lose, the reverse will happen. 46, 57

Racket—You will not enjoy a pleasure you anticipated. 97, 54

Radish—To see it growing is an omen of good luck. If you eat radishes, you will suffer disappointments through the thoughtlessness of a friend. 17, 42

Raffle—Losses through injudicious speculations. 67, 34

Raft—You will make a change of business location which will prove beneficial. If you float on one, you will make uncertain journeys. 29, 71

Rage—Quarrels and injuries to your friends if you see yourself in a rage. If you see someone else enraged, it denotes unfavorable conditions in your business and life in general. 79, 62

Railroad—If you see one, it indicates your business needs more attention, as you are in danger of losing it through the machinations of enemies. If you walk the rails, you will meet with successful ventures. 23, 80

Rain—If you dream of walking in the midst of clear rain, you will be blessed with pleasures and energetic vitality, as well as prosperity in all your affairs. 11, 97

Rainbow—Success and joy in all your affairs and unusual events that will bring you happiness. 42, 56

Raisins—If you eat them, your hopes will fail to materialize. 37, 63

Ram—Bad luck and troubles ahead. 15, 6

Ransom—Deceit is evident around you. A lot of people exploit your good will and take money from you. 86, 49

Rape—If a woman dreams of being raped, she will have love troubles and a possible separation from her lover. 17, 39

Raspberries—Beware of entanglements which may prove costly, even if interesting. 93, 2

Rat—You have deceitful neighbors. Beware lest you meet with injuries through them. If you kill a rat in a dream, you will succeed over all your enemies. 18, 74

Rattle—Happy home life and success in all your affairs. 83, 45

Razor—Arguments and troubles with relatives and associates. If you cut yourself with one, you will be unlucky in a new deal. 38, 24

Reading—If you dream you are reading, you will excel in a difficult task. If others are reading, you will find help in your friends whenever you need it. 35, 72

Reception—Pleasant engagements. 66, 81

Records—There may soon be a death in your family. 76, 43

Red—Beware of arguments. If you are dressed in red, you may soon enter into a passionate love affair. 55, 7

Refrigerator—You may hurt someone in his or her livelihood. 31, 9

Register—To register at a hotel indicates adventures and unexpected events. At the polls, a change in government. 11, 4

Reindeer—You will always be true to your friends and accept your responsibilities. 16, 82

Relative—You will soon receive bad news from someone close. 64, 88

Religion—Disagreements and separations in both love and business. 27, 67

Rent—If you rent a house, you will sign a profitable contract. To pay rent denotes your finances are in good condition. 39, 44

Reptiles—If you are attacked by one, you are faced

with serious troubles in business. If you kill it, you will succeed in overcoming all difficulties. 23, 75

Rescue—To be rescued in a dream means you will escape from a possible injury or a business difficulty. If you rescue another, you will be appreciated for your kindness to others. 13, 45

Resign—To resign a position indicates you will start new enterprises that will prove failures. If others resign, you will hear unpleasant news. 27, 56

Restaurant—Be careful of your diet and avoid excesses in any form. 78, 64

Resurrection—To dream you resurrect from the dead means you will have to face a great problem that you will eventually overcome. 14, 85

Revelation—If you receive a revelation in a dream and it is a happy one, you will be facing success soon. If it is not so pleasant, you may have obstacles to overcome. 96, 54

Revenge—Loss of friendship and danger from enemies. 23, 67

Revolver—Separations and disagreements. 89, 36

Rhinoceros—Great loss is possible soon. If you kill one, you will be able to overcome all obstacles. 27, 79

Rib—An omen of poverty. 76, 43

Ribbon—Gay and pleasant friends and companions. A happy life is predicted for you, if the ribbon is not black. 43, 29

Rice—Success and warm friendships to see it. To eat it indicates a happy home life and general prosperity. 77, 53

Riches—If you see yourself in the possession of

many riches, you will rise to a high position through hard work. 91, 35

Riddle—Confusion and dissatisfaction. 44, 8

Ride—This is an omen of sickness and bad business. 69, 18

Ring—To wear one denotes a new business that will prove a success. 33, 71

Riot—Disappointments in your affairs. A death among your friends is possible. 88, 2

Rival—To dream of having one indicates losses, through your own procrastination, in what should rightfully be yours. 46, 52

River—If it is clear and serene, it denotes happiness and many pleasures and overall prosperity. If the waters are turbulent or murky, you will be faced with jealousy and many arguments. 87, 36

Road—A rough, unknown road indicates new enterprises, which will bring you many losses. If it is smooth and bordered with foliage, you can expect good fortune and happiness in your life soon. If a friend walks with you, it denotes a good companion in life, a happy home and a congenial spouse. 55, 17

Roast—Troubles at home and deceit among your friends. 22, 76

Robber—You will receive an unexpected present. 90, 63

Rock—Happiness and good fortune after some hard work. 5, 99

Rocket—To see one ascending to the sky predicts you will rise to a high position and will succeed in winning the object of your affections. If the rocket falls, you will be unhappy in love and marriage. 86, 34

Rocking chair—If someone is rocking in it, you will enjoy much success and happiness at home, in love and business. If the rocking chair is empty, it portends separations and sadness. 77, 9, 12

Roof—To be on one indicates you will meet with great success in all your affairs. If you see a roof caving in, you will be faced with a great calamity. 27, 68

Rooster—You will reach a prominent position, but you will become arrogant and conceited as a result. To see roosters fighting indicates arguments and dissensions around you. 86, 46

Roots—A bad sign for both business and health if you see the roots of trees or plants. 27, 37

Ropes—Confusion and doubts in your life, especially in love. 41, 60

Rosary—Sorrows and troubles brought on by your own faults. 15, 6

Roses—To see or smell roses indicates great pleasures and success in all things, particularly in love. A happy marriage may come your way soon. If the roses are withered, they denote the absence of a loved one. 75, 83

Roulette—Struggles and strife with rivals and enemies. 48, 94

Rowboat—You will enjoy the company of many pleasant friends, if you see yourself in one with other people. If the boat capsizes, it denotes business losses. 57, 38

Rubber—To wear rubber clothes indicates honors

to come due to your honesty and integrity. To see rubber objects means secret business deals and a secretive life. 14, 8

Ruby—Lucky in business transactions and in love affairs. To lose one indicates love troubles. 85, 92

Ruins—Broken engagements between lovers and bad business deals. 16, 35

Rum—To drink it indicates you will achieve great wealth, but you will grow dissipated with time if you are not careful. 3, 74

Running—You will achieve riches and a high position. If you stumble or fall, you will suffer losses of both property and reputation. 65, 93

Rust—Sickness, misfortunes and false friends will be your lot. Be strong, as you will succeed if you but try. 42, 14

—S—

Sack—You will find some valuable object you thought was lost. 17, 20

Sacrifice—Many unexpected changes around you, not all for the best. 28, 71

Saddle—Pleasant news and unexpected visitors. A pleasant journey is also possible. 35, 12

Safe—To see one indicates security in business matters and also in love. 83, 71

Sailing—If you dream of sailing on calm waters,

you will find it easy to succeed in all things in life. 25, 47

Sailor—You will enjoy many happy and advantageous journeys. To a woman, this dream portends separation from her lover. 26, 40

Salad—To eat it indicates sickness to come, as well as nasty people around you. 76, 52

Salmon—Good fortune and pleasant occupations. To eat it predicts a happy marriage with a pleasant and congenial partner. 7, 57

Salt—Disagreeable surroundings frustrate your efforts to improve your life. To eat salt means you will be deserted by your lover for another person. 25, 38

Sand—An omen of hunger and poverty to come. 11, 63

Sanskrit—You will investigate occult subjects successfully. 17, 32

Sapphire—To see one is an omen of good fortune and many gains. 12, 9

Sardines—To eat them indicates you will be faced with distressing events. 66, 18

Satan—Beware of flattery and immorality to achieve your aim. If you overcome him, you will find the inner strength to overcome dangerous temptations. 15, 80

Sausage—To make it means you will succeed in all your affairs. If you eat a sausage in a dream, you will have a happy home, albeit humble. 34, 76

Saw—To use one indicates you will have a lot of work to do, as well as a happy home life. To see a saw is also a lucky omen, predicting a successful business. 62, 89

Sawdust—A serious mistake will cause a lot of trouble for you at home. 31, 94

Scaffold—Many disappointments in love. To descend one portends you will commit a legal offense and will pay for it. 13, 8

Scales—You will find prosperity through your just and fair handling of your affairs. 28, 64

Scandal—To be the object of scandal denotes you should be careful in your choice of friends or companions, as they could cause you troubles later on. 15, 68

Sceptre—To wield one means you will be chosen to occupy positions of responsibility and great merit, which you will fulfill honorably. If others wield the sceptre, you will work under others. 29, 46

School—To attend it portends literary honors. To teach in school means you will aspire to those honors but must first work as a means of survival. 16, 3

Scissors—Jealousy and quarrels between lovers or husband and wife. 77, 64

Scorpions—Beware of enemies and false friends who will try to take advantage of you. 17, 58

Scratch—Beware of enemies trying to cause you harm or destroy your property. 16, 92

Scream—You have enemies who are attempting to harm you. 88, 15

Screen—You will attempt to hide your faults and mistake behind a false front. It will not work, so do not bother trying. 37, 49

Screw—You must perform tiresome tasks for little gain. 14, 23

Sculptor—You will change your line of work to something less profitable but more distinguished. 58, 69

Scythe—Beware of accidents and sickness. 15, 28

Sea—To hear the waves breaking indicates a lonely life without the love of a faithful companion. Also unfulfilled desires. 67, 30

Seal—You have high ambitions and will do anything to achieve them. 27, 46

Seamstress—You will not be able to make a much-planned visit due to unexpected happenings. 37, 58

Seat—Security and protection in life. 17, 84

Secret—An unexpected fortune will soon come your way. 67, 5

Secretary—You will soon receive unexpected good news. 29, 48

Seducer—You will be influenced by loud and artful people. 56, 92

Seed—You will soon meet with prosperity, even if your present situation is rather poor. 25, 70

Serenade—You will receive pleasant news from distant friends. 7, 32

Servant—Good fortune is coming your way, in spite of negative conditions at present. Beware of anger, as it can cause unnecessary quarrels. 34, 92

Sewing—Domestic peace and harmony will surround you. 22, 93

Sex—To engage in sex with your spouse or lover indicates fruitful unions and attainment of desires. If a stranger is your sex partner, beware of public disgrace and losses. 18, 62

Sexual organs—You will receive a large sum of money soon. 33, 75

Shadow—Beware of an enemy who is plotting to hurt you. 14, 88

Shampoo—To shampoo your hair indicates you will soon rid yourself of many unwarranted problems and worries. To see a lot of lather is a warning against false illusions. 78, 52

Shark—Beware of enemies and secret jealousies and envy. 89, 24

Shave—You will succeed in all your business ventures. 97, 2

Sheep—If they are fat and healthy, much happiness and prosperity is in store for you. If they are lean and hungry, they predict unhappiness through the failure of a business venture. 81, 35

Shelf—If they are empty, they prognosticate losses and bad luck. If they are full, you will achieve your fondest wishes. 27, 43

Shelter—To find it you will escape from the machinations of evil people. If you are searching for shelter, beware of causing mischief and then trying to escape punishment. 17, 68

Sheriff—Uncertainty through unexpected changes. 23, 87

Ship—Honors and distinctions. A shipwreck predicts a disastrous turn of events. If the ship struggles through a storm, you will have difficulties in your affairs. 34, 75

Shirt—A bad omen predicting separations from loved ones, misfortunes and general unhappiness.

If the shirt is dirty, beware of contagious diseases. 58, 90

Shoe—Your critical attitude will make you a lot of enemies if you are not more discreet in expressing your opinions. New shoes are an indication of improvements in your life. 11, 65

Shooting—Unhappiness in love or in your married life. 17, 43

Shop—To see one denotes you have jealous friends who will scheme to spoil your chances of success. 14, 82

Shoulder—Other people's shoulders indicate happy changes that will transform your way of thinking. 8, 75

Shovel—Hard work that will bear fruit. If the shovel is broken, you will have losses. 46, 32

Shower—To be in one denotes an interest in refined pleasures. You possess a fine intellect and creative talents. 24, 7

Shrimp—You will soon take a pleasurable journey. 44, 72

Shroud—Sickness and anxiety as a result of it. Beware of deceitful friends. Business decline is threatened. 21, 69

Sickness—Trouble and real sickness are forthcoming. 36, 82

Sigh—Sadness is forthcoming but it will eventually be overcome by fine prospects. 34, 57

Silk—High ambitions will be gratified. Reconciliations between estranged lovers. 19, 63

Silver—Worries and unsatisfied desires. Beware of depending too much on money for true happiness and peace. 46, 94

Singing—Happy news from someone far away, and the company of cheerful friends. 37, 84

Sister—Much luck and happiness will come your way. 22, 61

Sister-in-law—Arguments in the family. 33, 98

Skate—To see skates indicates dissension among your associates. To see young people skating denotes good health and pleasure in helping others. 56, 41

Skeleton—Illness, misunderstanding and possible injuries at the hands of others. If one chases you, it is an omen of death or business. 27, 81

Skin—An omen of good fortune to come. 13, 10

Skirt—Flirtations and frivolous pastimes. 54, 71

Skull—Domestic quarrels and difficulties. Beware of business troubles. 78, 49

Sky—Many honors and distinguished friends. Pleasant trips and many, many pleasures, but only if the sky is clear. If it is cloudy or grey, you will not see your hopes realized. 51, 89

Slaughterhouse—You will be more feared than loved by your lover or spouse. 52, 64

Sleep—To sleep in pleasant surroundings indicates peace and favors from those you love. If the sleeping place is not nice, you will soon face sickness and broken engagements. 76, 45

Sleigh—Beware of making erroneous judgments in business or love. 78, 92

Sliding—Disappointments in love and business. 61, 23

Slippers—You will make an unwise business deal and it will backfire on you, if you are not careful.

Beware also of secret and dangerous love affairs. 63, 28

Smile—You will soon find new joys to relieve past sorrows. 45, 72

Smoke—Doubts and fears will cloud your life, if you allow them. Beware of flattery and deceitful persons. 42, 36

Snail—Unhealthful conditions around you. 18, 45

Snake—An evil omen predicting danger through enemies, deceit and general misfortunes. If you kill the snakes, you will overcome all obstacles. 71, 98

Sneeze—Hasty news will make you change your plans. 16, 53

Snow—Sorrows and disappointments, especially if you see yourself in the midst of a snowstorm. 26, 79

Soap—Success and enjoyable times to come. 67, 91

Soldier—You should be careful in making decisions, as they may alter the course of your life. 54, 39

Son—If you see your son well and happy, he will attain honors and make you very happy. If you see him ill or hurt in any way, there is trouble in the near future. 61, 48

Sores—Losses through illness. 14, 82

Soup—You will enjoy many pleasures and comforts. 72, 46

Sowing—To sow seed foretells fruitful times to come with many business gains. 65, 98

Spades—Unwise deals will bring you much distress and misfortune. 29, 40

Sparrow—You will be surrounded by much love and comfort. If the sparrow is hurt or wounded, you will experience sadness in the near future. 76, 50

Speaking—You will enjoy life and many comforts in late life. 76, 5

Spear—A happy home life and many comforts in late life. 76, 5

Spice—Beware you do not hurt your reputation through your love of pleasures. 14, 88

Spider—Your hard work will result in an agreeable fortune. A spider web indicates security of home and family. To kill one predicts quarrels at home or between lovers. 77, 12

Spit—Disagreements and unhappy endings to promising undertakings. 97, 61

Splinter—Troubles through relatives or jealous rivals. 24, 87

Sponge—Deception and lies around you. 14, 54

Spool—Spools of thread indicate a long and difficult road ahead with much hard work and troubles, but culminating in great success. 17, 16

Spoon—Advancement in your affairs and a happy home life. If the spoon is soiled or broken, beware of losses and disappointments. 27, 8

Spring—Fortunate undertakings and pleasant companions. 1, 92

Spy—Dangerous quarrels and estrangements. 29, 10

Squirrel—Pleasant friends and business gains. If you kill it, you will face unpopularity and loss of friends. 35, 19

Stable—Good fortune to come. 12, 77

Stain—Troubles over small matters. Stains on others predicts someone will betray you. 13, 4

Stairs—Good fortune and happiness and honors if you see or climb them. If you fall down or climb down the stairs, you will be unlucky in love and general affairs, and will be the object of envy and hatred. 25, 74

Stallion—Prosperity and honors will be yours. 19, 1

Stammer—Worries and illness will beset you. 26, 7

Stars—Good health and prosperity. A shooting or falling star denotes sadness and sorrows. 32, 73

Starving—Unfruitful labors and loss of friends if you see yourself starving. To see others starve predicts poverty and dissatisfaction with your friends or companions. 24, 17

Statue—Separation from a loved one. Lack of energy will impede your business progress. 76, 51

Steal—To dream of stealing or seeing others steal portends bad luck and misunderstandings. 67, 41

Stepfather—Good fortune and many business gains. 31, 8

Stepmother—Death may be near. 15, 98

Steps—To ascend them predicts honors and prosperity will overcome your present anxiety. To descend them portends further problems in your business affairs. 14, 58

Stethoscope—Your hopes will not be realized. Troubles in love affairs. 37, 24

Stew—You will have a large financial gain. 12, 7

Stockings—Beware of immorality and dissolute companions. 13, 4

Stone—Many confusions and failures. To throw a

stone indicates you will reprimand someone. 43, 16

Store—Prosperity and advancements in all affairs. 3, 75

Storm—Sickness and unfavorable business deals. Also foretells separation between friends. 14, 66

Straw—Emptiness and failure in your life. If the straw is burning, it is a sign of victory over difficulties and of prosperity to come. 17, 56

Strawberries—Many gains and pleasures in life. You will get a long-desired thing. To eat them means your love will be returned. 67, 81

Street—Bad luck and worries over your hopes and plans. Any trips you undertake now will not be as pleasurable or beneficial as you expected. 52, 6

Student—Danger in the streets for one of your family. 11, 25

Suffocate—Sorrow and distress through the conduct of someone you love. Be careful with your health. 28, 14

Sugar—Unpleasantness around you which will dissipate after some time. Beware of jealousies and petty worries. 16, 39

Suicide—If you commit suicide in a dream, you will soon meet with misfortune. If others meet this fate, it denotes the failure of others will affect your affairs. 66, 51

Sulphur—Be careful with your affairs, as someone is planning to hurt you. If you eat the sulphur, you will enjoy good health and many satisfactions in life in general. 81, 92

Sun—Many happy events and prosperity to come. A sunset indicates you should take care of your interests, as they are in the wane. 24, 72

Surgeon—Beware of enemies connected with your business. To women this dream predicts a serious illness. 73, 49

Surgical instruments—Dissatisfaction with your friends. 54, 80

Surprise—Hasty news by letter will bring an unexpected announcement. 56, 93

Swamp—Adversity and distress in your life. Disappointments in your love life. If the swamp has clear water and greenery surrounds it, you will eventually gain much prosperity and success after much intrigue and conniving. 16, 89

Swan—If it swims upon placid waters, you will enjoy prosperity and many pleasures. A dead swan foretells dissatisfaction in love and life in general. 13, 99

Swearing—You will meet with many obstacles in business. 63, 28

Sweeping—Pleasures and happiness in the home and in family life. 12, 46

Sweetheart—You will meet a marriage partner who will bring both emotional and financial rewards to your life. 73, 26

Swelling—You will succeed in accumulating a large future, but be careful that selfishness will not spoil your enjoyment of it. 29, 35

Swimming—If the swimming is pleasant and effortless, you will meet with much success. Otherwise, you will have dissatisfactions in your business deals. 62, 85

Sword—High position with many honors and distinction, if you own the sword. If others brandish swords, it denotes quarrels and disagreements. 27, 15

Symphony—Many delightful things to do. 12, 5

Syringe—False alarm about someone's illness. That person is less sick than is believed. If syringe is broken, illness is near. 48, 71

—T—

Table—A table set for a meal predicts many happy unions and prosperity. If it is empty, there will be poverty and arguments in the future. 11, 83

Tail—To see the tail of an animal indicates annoyances where pleasures were expected. 17, 62

Tailor—Worries through a journey that you will make. 32, 41

Talisman—Pleasant friends and help from powerful people. 51, 86

Talking—Worries over the illness of a relative and over your business affairs. 72, 69

Tangerine—You will escape injury through the help of others. 78, 40

Tank—Prosperity and satisfaction in all your affairs. 82, 95

Tar—Beware of dangerous enemies and pitfalls in business. To get it on your hands is an indication of sickness and distress. 95, 48

Tarantula—Enemies may overwhelm you if you do not take care. To kill one indicates overcoming of difficulties. 97, 53

Target—Much responsibility will take your mind away from enjoyment of pleasures. Beware of deceit around you. 91, 52

Tattoo—You will be forced to go away from home for a prolonged stay due to an unexpected difficulty. Tattoos on others predict jealousies through unusual loves. 13, 58

Taxes—To pay them indicates you will overcome negative influences around you. 89, 46

Taxi—You will receive a hasty message. 8, 71

Tea—Unforeseen difficulties in your affairs. 39, 26

Teacher—An invitation to an important festivity. 16, 48

Teeth—To see teeth predicts sickness to come and disagreeable people. To see your teeth falling out foretells death, and grief will come to you soon. 13, 98

Telegram—You will soon receive disagreeable news. 94, 36

Telephone—Much jealousy and envy surround you, but you will triumph over all odds. 17, 58

Telescope—Difficult times to come for love and business. To see planets through one portends much pleasure through traveling. 16, 81

Tent—Changes in your affairs. 76, 43

Theater—Much satisfaction in your affairs and joy through friends. 37, 59

Thermometer—Unsatisfactory business deals and troubles in the home. Illness is forthcoming if you see one broken. 7, 62

Thief—If you are a thief in a dream, you will meet reverses in your affairs. If you pursue or capture one, you will have victory over your enemies. 99, 74

Thigh—Good luck and pleasure, if it is healthy. If wounded or lame, beware of deceit and illness. 25, 47

Thimble—You will have to take care of a lot of other people. If you lose one, beware of poverty and distress. 87, 63

Thirst—You aspire to things that are beyond your reach. If you quench your thirst in a dream, you will reach your aspirations. 91, 73

Thorns—Difficulties impede your success. Beware of hidden enemies. 17, 66

Thread—Your luck must be pursued in complicated ways. Broken threads indicate losses through faithless friends. 35, 61

Throat—An attractive throat indicates a swift rise in position. A sore throat portends deception through a friend. 18, 57

Throne—If you sit on one, you will reach high honors and distinctions. To see others on a throne means you will gain riches through the help of others. 90, 85

Thumb—An uncertain future lies ahead, but you will find much help among artistic and creative people. 88, 74

Thunder—Reverses in business, and grief to someone close to you. 65, 48

Tiger—Much persecution through enemies. Failure

if it attacks and hurts you. If you kill it, you will over-come all opposition. 38, 73

Tobacco—Success in business but unhappiness in love matters. 16, 56

Toilet—Your shyness can cause you a lot of losses in business and your general affairs. 71, 62

Tomatoes—If you eat them, good health and do-mestic happiness. 65, 49

Tomb—Sadness and business disappointments. 83, 50

Tongue—To see your own tongue denotes you will find ill favor with your acquaintances. If the tongue of another, you will meet with scandals and vilifica-tion. 32, 79

Topaz—Much good fortune and pleasant com-panions. 17, 68

Torch—Pleasant endeavors and gains in business. 11, 92

Tornado—Disappointments in business and troubles at home. 27, 63

Torture—To be tortured indicates disappointment and sorrows through the deceit of false friends. If you torture others, you will fail to carry out certain plans that could ensure your fortunes for life. 84, 76

Tourist—To be one means you will travel far from your home base and find much enjoyment during this trip. To see tourists indicates love anxieties and poor business. 36, 59

Tower—To see one indicates high ambitions. If you ascend one, your hopes will be realized. 68, 47

Toys—Happy home life if they are new. If old or broken, death will fill your life with grief. 71, 68

Train—To see a train indicates you will soon make a journey. If you are in the train and it is moving smoothly, you will accomplish your plans and realize your hopes. 26, 55

Traitor—Enemies will try to destroy you. 8, 94

Trap—If you are caught in one, you will be overcome by enemies. To see an empty trap denotes misfortune in the near future. 24, 71

Travel—Profits combined with pleasure. To travel in a crowded car indicates happy adventures with congenial friends. 67, 8

Treasure—To find one denotes good luck in finding someone to help you achieve your goals in life. To lose one indicates business losses are forthcoming. 23, 97

Tree—Green trees foretell realized hopes and desires fulfilled. If they are dead or fallen, indicates losses and grief. To climb a tree denotes prestige and distinctions will come to you. 17, 63

Triangle—Separation from friends and the end of love affairs through bitter quarrels. 27, 81

Trousers—Temptation to commit errors that could result in dishonor. 72, 58

Trumpet—To see one indicates an unusual event is about to take place in your life. If you blow one, you will achieve your fondest wishes. 46, 83

Trunk—Journeys and bad luck to come. If you pack one, you will soon go on a pleasant trip. 18, 70

Tub—A tub full of water indicates a happy home life. If it is empty, it denotes family quarrels and disagreements. 25, 38

Tunnel—To go through one is a signal of bad luck in

business and love. To look inside one denotes worries to come. 43, 97

Turkey—Gains in business and improvements in your affairs. If you eat it, you will enjoy many happy occasions soon. 56, 39

Turquoise—You will soon realize a fond wish. 67, 42

Turtle—An unusual event will bring you much happiness and business gains. 73, 81

Tweezers—Uncomfortable situations will distress and upset your life. 65, 99

Twins—Business gains and a happy home life. 54, 28

Typhoid—If you suffer from typhoid, it means you should beware of hidden enemies. A typhoid epidemic indicates business losses and poor health are threatened. 88, 71

—U—

Ugly—If you see yourself ugly, you will have love troubles. 8, 68

Ulcer—Loss of friends and separation from loved ones. 33, 54

Umbrella—To shelter yourself under an umbrella during a shower is an omen of happiness and prosperity. To carry one denotes troubles and worries. To use a leaky one indicates disappointments in love and friendship. 97, 62

Uncle—Sad news is soon forthcoming. 79, 50

Undertaker—You will receive news about a wedding. 77, 57

Undress—To undress in a dream indicates people will talk badly about you behind your back. 61, 20

Uniform—To see one indicates powerful friends will help you reach your highest objectives in life. 34, 17

Urine—To see it is an indication of poor health and troubles with your friend. To urinate in a dream denotes bad luck and love difficulties. 88, 47

—V—

Vacation—This year will prove to be prosperous and happy for you. 78, 54

Vaccination—Dissatisfaction in your affairs and problems with your love life. 7, 62

Valentine—To send one indicates lost opportunities to enrich yourself. To receive one predicts a weak but passionate marriage partner. 44, 82

Valley—Green valleys predict business improvements and love joys. The opposite is predicted if the valley is dry and desolate. 32, 74

Vampire—You will have marital troubles sparked by greed. 18, 74

Vapor—Depressing companions around you. 91, 27

Varnish—You will achieve honors through fraud. 31, 9

Vase—To see one indicates happiness at home. To drink from one portends you will steal someone's lover away from them. A broken one predicts grief to come. 16, 31

Vatican—Unexpected honors from important people. 23, 98

Vault—Grief and misfortunes. Beware of deceit around you. If the vault is filled with your valuables, you will make a fortune surprising many people. 11, 79

Vegetables—Unexpected good luck coming your way, if you eat them. If they are rotten or dried, you will meet with much sadness. 18, 95

Veil—To wear one denotes insincerity and deceit. A bridal or a beautiful veil is an indication of successful changes in the near future. If others wear veils, beware of deceitful friends. 76, 40

Vein—To see your own veins indicates protection against slander. If they are bleeding, you can expect grief and misfortune. 8, 47

Velvet—Success in all business deals. To wear it denotes honors to come. 75, 39

Ventriloquist—Beware of treachery around you. 65, 81

Vicar—Beware of jealousy and envy, lest they lead you into foolish actions. 22, 94

Vice—Do not endanger your reputation by listening to evil companions. 30, 6

Victim—To be one indicates you are in danger of being overpowered by your enemies. Family troubles are also indicated. 49, 2

Victory—You will successfully overpower your enemies and enjoy much pleasure in love. 5, 75

Vine—Prosperity and success are indicated, as well as good health for some time to come. 26, 78

Vinegar—To drink it denotes distress through a disagreeable undertaking. This dream is a bad omen in all respects. 8, 68

Violence—If you are the victim, you will be overcome by enemies. If you are the victimizer, you will lose much through your wasteful and negative behavior. 18, 53

Violets—Happy occasions to come and the love of a truly wonderful person. 55, 77

Violin—To see or hear one indicates peace and harmony around you, as well as gains in business. 73, 26

Viper—Calamities threaten you, unless you kill the viper. In this case, you will escape without harm from dangers around you. 83, 94

Virgin—Good luck in all your affairs. 58, 31

Visit—To visit someone in a dream denotes happy occupations in the near future. If the visit is unpleasant, beware of deceitful or malicious persons. 88, 46

Voice—To hear voices in a dream predicts happy reconciliations, so long as the voices are pleasant. Disappointments otherwise. 28, 14

Volcano—To see one in eruption indicates violent arguments and dissensions. 69, 35

Vomit—You will be faced with an illness that may prove costly, or with a great scandal, if you are vomiting. To see someone else vomiting indicates you will become aware of the deceit of someone you trust. 16, 48

Vote—To dream of voting indicates involvement in a community problem. 29, 73

Vow—To make or listen to vows denotes complaints will be launched against you for unlawful business practices. Love affairs are also threatened. 24, 79

Voyage—An inheritance is in store for you. 11, 9

Vulture—A deceitful person is out to hurt you. If the vulture is dead, you will succeed in overcoming this individual. 87, 61

—W—

Wading—If the water is clear, you will experience wonderful joys. If it is muddy, beware of illness or grief. 16, 38

Wafer—A bad omen indicating loss of fortune and dangers through enemies. 1, 46

Wages—To receive them is an indication of helpful friends. To pay them is a sign of growing dissatisfaction. 22, 67

Wagon—A sign of an unhappy marriage to come. A broken one is a sign of sadness and misfortune. But to drive one uphill indicates an improvement in your affairs. 7, 55

Waist—Good fortune to come. 17, 39

Waiter—A friend will provide you with pleasant entertainment. 7, 54

Walking—To walk through pleasant places indicates good fortune and favor from important people. To walk at night denotes misfortune to come. 91, 25

Wallet—Pleasant responsibilities that you will enjoy handling. 10, 53

Walls—If they obstruct your path, beware of bad influences that may prove costly. If you jump over them, you will overcome all obstacles in your life and accomplish all your plans. 21, 70

Walnut—Joys and favors from important persons. 1, 82

Waltz—To see someone else dancing indicates happy relationships with congenial friends. To dance with someone, especially with your lover, indicates sexual pleasures and a passionate love affair with that person. 10, 7

War—Difficult conditions in business and in your affairs in general. 92, 57

Warehouse—A new enterprise which will prove successful. If it is empty, beware of being cheated in a plan you are carefully devising. 12, 58

Warts—If you have them, you will be the victim of attacks upon your honor. To see warts on someone else indicates bitter enemies prepare to harm you. 18, 72

Washing—One of your close friends will be in much trouble through evil gossip. 25, 87

Wasp—Beware of the attacks of enemies against you. If you are stung by one, you will be the victim of jealousy and envy. 79, 63

Watch—To see one means prosperity in all your affairs. To check the time on a watch indicates you will be overcome by rivals. 35, 20

Water—Clear water indicates prosperity and happiness to come. Muddy or turbulent water is a sign of dangers and misfortunes. To drink muddy water portends illness to come. To play with water predicts sudden passion and love. 10, 7

Waterfall—You will attain your fondest wish. 51, 70

Waves—You are planning to take an important step and will succeed if the water is clear. Failure is predicted if the water is muddy or cloudy. 9, 47

Wealth—You will overcome all problems through will power and determination. To see others wealthy indicates you will have good friends who will help you in times of need. 14, 61

Weather—Fluctuations in life. 38, 92

Weaving—You will overcome all problems in your life and will succeed in building a fortune. 73, 46

Web—Beware of deceitful friends who will try to destroy your plans. 82, 77

Wedding—To attend one indicates delayed success and many worries. To see your own means you will meet with much grief and a possible death in your family. 65, 47

Wedding ring—If you see your own wedding band looking bright and shiny, you will have a loving, caring companion for life. If it is lost or broken, you will suffer in life through death or incompatibility with your mate. 23, 88

Well—To draw water from one indicates fulfillment of all your desires. To see one empty or to fall into one indicates suffering and misfortunes. 87, 37

Wet—To dream of being wet indicates pleasures that could involve you in loss and scandal. 73, 54

Whale—To see one denotes many problems to come and the threat of property loss. 18, 65

Wheat—Fields of ripe wheat predict great fortune and prosperity as well as faithful love. 76, 41

Whip—Quarrels and separations in families. 38, 71

Whirlpool—Dangers in business through intrigues. 86, 53

Whirlwind—You are facing a calamitous change in your life that could bring you great unhappiness. 8, 32

Whisky—To see it in bottles denotes protection of your interests. To drink it predicts struggling to achieve a goal and accomplishing it only after many disappointments. 6, 44

Whisper—Evil gossip around you. 11, 3

Whistle—Sad news will cause you to change pleasurable plans. If you whistle, you will enjoy many pleasurable moments. 75, 39

Widow—To dream of being one indicates much distress through malicious persons. 32, 69

Wife—Disagreements and arguments in the home. 88, 93

Wig—To wear one indicates you will soon make a bad change in your life. If others are wearing wigs, you are surrounded by deceitful persons. 66, 42

Will—To make one denotes many difficult decisions

and troubles to come. 53, 28

Wind—If the wind blows softly on you, a great inheritance will be yours through a death. A brisk wind foretells you will overcome temptations and achieve a fortune and status in the world through hard work and determination. 55, 91

Windmill—Happiness and prosperity to come. 53, 26

Window—Fruitless enterprises and wasted hopes are in store for you. 48, 60

Wine—To drink it denotes joy and good friends. To see barrels of wine foretells luxury and prosperity. 57, 71

Wings—To have wings denotes you will fear for the safety of a loved one who is far away from you. To dream of the wings of birds or fowl indicates you will have to struggle through much adversity but will eventually succeed. 55, 9

Winter—Bad health and difficult times to come. 49, 27

Wire—Beware of your bad temper and do not take any chances with your business deals, as trickery could be near. 64, 79

Witch—Be careful with your business and your home life. 14, 68

Witness—To be a witness against others is an omen of depression and troubles to come. If others bear witness against you, it means strain on friendships through lack of cooperation on your part. 75, 41

Wolf—You may employ a thief or a talebearer. The howl of a wolf indicates some people are allied to defeat you in a business competition. 24, 38

Women—Intrigues and losses, if you are not careful. 8, 79

Wood—A scandal may threaten you and your family. 59, 7

Woods—Changes in your affairs which will be good if the woods are green, and bad if they are dry or stripped of their foliage. A wood on fire indicates your plans will be completed successfully as planned. 12, 45

Wool—You will have the opportunity to achieve your greatest dreams. 27, 59

Work—You will succeed in life through determination and energy, if you see yourself working. To see others at work you will have positive conditions around you. 67, 12

Worm—Beware of intrigues on the part of disreputable persons. To use them as bait predicts you will use your enemies to advance your own affairs. 81, 20

Wound—To be wounded indicates difficulties in business. To see others wounded means you will be the victim of an injustice by a friend. 34, 61

Wreath—Great opportunities will present themselves for enriching yourself. 10, 78

Wreck—You will fear difficulties in business or destitution. 16, 4

Writing—To write indicates you will make a mistake which will prove costly. To see writing foretells the possibility of a lawsuit against you. 59, 32

—X—

X rays—Beware of fires and of getting burned. 90, 67

Xylophone—Happy times are soon forthcoming. If you play one, you will be in control of your life and will succeed beyond all your expectations. 7, 69

—Y—

Yacht—Happy recreations away from business. 71, 90

Yardstick—You are a hypercritical individual and your friends and acquaintances resent it. 47, 25

Yarn—Success in your business deals and a happy home life. 19, 3

Yawn—Dissatisfaction with your life in general. 32, 60

Yeast—The opportunity will present itself where you can make a great deal of money. 16, 83

Yelling—Troubles in business through carelessness. 56, 82

Yellow—Happiness and satisfaction in your affairs. 5, 19

Yoke—You will conform unwillingly to the tastes and habits of others. 38, 64

Yolk—You will have good luck in games of chance in the near future. 64, 98

Young—Reconciliation among family members. A good time to start new enterprises. 12, 70

—Z—

Zebra—You are interested in enterprises that can offer no security for the future. 3, 48

Zenith—Great prosperity and a wealthy, loving marriage partner. 7, 59

Zephyr—You will sacrifice much in the pursuit of your true love and will find your love amply returned. 86, 93

Zero—Do not be disturbed by trifling problems. 27, 64

Zinc—Substantial and powerful progress in your affairs. 97, 45

Zodiac—Great success in all your affairs, as well as peace and happiness in your personal life. 38, 49

Zombie—You are being misled by deceitful people. You must try to exert a greater control over your own life. 72, 31

Zoo—Gains through travels. Many ups and downs in your affairs in general. 13, 7

THE LLEWELLYN ANNUALS

Llewellyn's MOON SIGN BOOK: Approximately 400 pages of valuable information on gardening, fishing, weather, stock market forecasts, personal horoscopes, good planting dates, and instructions for finding the best date to do just about anything! Articles by prominent forecasters and writers in the fields of gardening, astrology, politics, economics and cycles. Fun, informative—a great help to millions in their daily planning.   **State year $4.95**

Llewellyn's SUN SIGN BOOK: Your personal horoscope for the entire year! All 12 signs are included in one handy book. Also included are forecasts, special feature articles, and an action guide for each sign. Monthly horoscopes are written by Gloria Star, author of *Optimum Child*, for your personal Sun Sign. Articles on a variety of subjects written by well-known astrologers from around the country. Much more than just a horoscope guide! Entertaining and fun the year around.   **State year $4.95**

Llewellyn's DAILY PLANETARY GUIDE and ASTROLOGER'S DATEBOOK: Includes all major daily aspects plus their exact times in Eastern and Pacific time zones, lunar phases, signs and voids plus their times, planetary motion, a monthly ephemeris, sunrise and sunset tables, special articles on the planets, signs, aspects, a business guide, planetary hours, rulerships, and more. 5 1/4 x 8 format for more writing space, spiral bound to lay flat, address and phone listings, time zone conversion chart and blank horoscope chart.   **State year $6.95**

Llewellyn's ASTROLOGICAL CALENDAR: Large 52-pages wall calendar. Full color cover and color inside. Includes feature articles by famous astrologers, introductory information on astrology. Lunar Gardening Guide, celestial phenomena, a blank horoscope chart for your own chart data, and monthly date pages which include aspects, lunar information, planetary motion, ephemeris, personal forecasts, lucky dates, planting and fishing dates, and more. 10 x 13 size. Set in Central time, with conversion table for other time zones worldwide.   **State year $9.95**

SECRETS OF GYPSY FORTUNETELLING
by Ray Buckland

This book unveils the Romani secrets of fortunetelling, explaining in detail the many different methods used by these nomads. For generations they have survived on their skills as seers. Their accuracy is legendary. They are a people who seem to be born with "the sight" . . . the ability to look into the past, present and future using only the simplest of tools to aid them. Here you will learn to read palms, to interpret the symbols in a teacup, to read cards . . . both the Tarot and regular playing cards. Here are revealed the secrets of interpreting the actions of animals, of reading the weather, of recognizing birthmarks and the shape of hands. Impress your friends with your knowledge of many of these lesser Mysteries; uncommon forms of fortunetelling known only to a few.

ISBN: 0-87542-051-6, mass market, 220 pgs., illus. $3.95

THE COMPLETE BOOK OF
SPELLS, CEREMONIES & MAGIC
by Migene González-Wippler

This book is far more than a historical survey of magical techniques throughout the world. It is the most complete book of spells, ceremonies and magic ever assembled. It is the spiritual record of humanity.

Topics in this book include magical spells and rituals from virtually every continent and every people. The spells described are for love, wealth, success, protection, and health. Also examined are the theories and history of magic, including its evolution, the gods, the elements, the Kabbalah, the astral plane, ceremonial magic, famous books of magic and famous magicians. You will learn about talismanic magic, exorcisms and how to use the *I Ching*, how to interpret dreams, how to construct and interpret a horoscope, how to read Tarot cards, how to read palms, how to do numerology, and much more. Included are explicit instructions for love spells and talismans; spells for riches and money; weight-loss spells; magic for healing; psychic self-defense; spells for luck in gambling, and much more.

0-87542-286-1, 384 pages, 6 x 9, illus., softcover. $12.95

A KABBALAH FOR THE MODERN WORLD
by Migene González-Wippler

The Kabbalah is the basic form of Western mysticism, and this is an excellent manual of traditional Kabbalistic Magick! This book covers a variety of Kabbalistic topics including: Creation, the nature of God, the soul and soul mates, the astral and other planes, the four worlds, the history of the Kabbalah, Bible interpretation and more.

In this book Wippler shows that the ancient Kabbalists predicted the New Physics. She discusses such topics as: Planck's Quantum Theory, God and Light, Archetypes, Synchronicity, The Collective Unconscious, the Lemaitre 'Big Bang' Theory, Einstein's Theory of Relativity and much more.

0-87542-294-2, 240 pgs, 5¼ x 8, illus., softcover.   **$8.95**

The Truth About Witchcraft Today
by Scott Cunningham

This is a book written for the non-practitioner. It is intended to inform the public about the true nature of Wicca and to explode the myths often associated with it.

Religion is perhaps the most personal sphere of our lives. Because of this, much confusion exists between members of different religions.

There are those who use religion to oppress others, to vanquish civil rights and to suppress freedom of thought. This is exactly what has occurred to Witchcraft practitioners in the last 500 years. The public image of Witchcraft is falsely confused with murder, orgies, drug use and something called "Satanism."

Witchcraft is far different. It is Wicca—a religion, and folk magic—a natural practice. Hundreds of thousands of rational, sane persons are worshipping Goddesses and Gods unknown to outsiders. Many thousands of people are discovering how to utilize natural energies to create specific, positive changes in their lives. This book is an attempt to explode the myths about two practices which have been with us from the beginning of human thought. It is, indeed, *The Truth About Witchcraft Today*.

ISBN: 0-87542-127-X, mass market, 224 pgs.,   **$3.95**

CRYSTAL AWARENESS
by Catherine Bowman

For millions of years, crystals have been waiting for people to discover their wonderful powers. Today they are used in watches, computer chips and communication devices. But there is also a spiritual, holistic aspect to crystals.

Crystal Awareness will teach you everything you need to know about crystals to begin working with them. It will also help those who have been working with them to complete their knowledge. Topics include:

•Colored and Colorless Crystals•Single Points, Clusters and Double Terminated Crystals•Crystal and Human Energy Fields•Crystals as Energy Generators•Crystal Cleansing and Programming•Crystal Meditation•The Value of Polished Crystals•Crystals and Personal Spiritual Growth•Crystals and Chakras•How to Make Crystal Jewelry•Color Healing •Compatible Crystals and Metals•Several Crystal Healing Techniques, including The Star of David Healing•

Crystal Awareness is destined to be the guide of choice for people who are beginning their investigation of crystals.
0-87542-058-3, illustrated, softcover   **$3.95**

CRYSTAL HEALING: The Next Step
by Phyllis Galde

Discover the further secrets of quartz crystal! Now modern research and use have shown that crystals have even more healing and therapeutic properties than has been realized. Learn why polished, smoothed crystal is better to use to heighten your intuition, improve creativity and for healing.

Learn to use crystals for reprogramming your subconscious to eliminate problems and negative attitudes that prevent success. Here are techniques that people have successfully used—not just theories.

This book reveals newly discovered abilities of crystal now accessible to all, and is a sensible approach to crystal use. *Crystal Healing* will be your guide to improve the quality of your life and expand your consciousness.
0-87542-246-2, 240 pages, illus., photos, mass market   **$3.95**

MAGICAL HERBALISM: The Secret Craft of the Wise
by Scott Cunningham

In Magical Herbalism, certain plants are prized for the special range of energies—the vibrations, or powers—they possess. Magical Herbalism unites the powers of plants and man to produce, and direct, change in accord with human will and desire.

This is the Magic of amulets and charms, sachets and herbal pillows, incenses and scented oils, simples and infusions and anointments. It's Magic as old as our knowledge of plants, an art that anyone can learn and practice, and once again enjoy as we look to the Earth to rediscover our roots and make inner connections with the world of Nature.

This is the Magic of Enchantment . . . of word and gesture to shape the images of mind and channel the energies of the herbs. It is a Magic for *veryone*—for the herbs are easily and readily obtained, the tools are familiar or easily made, and the technology that of home and garden.

This book includes step-by-step guidance to the preparation of herbs and to their compounding in incense and oils, sachets and amulets, simples and infusions, with simple rituals and spells for every purpose.

0-87542-120-2, 256 pgs., 5¼ x 8, illus., softcover $7.95

THE MAGICAL HOUSEHOLD
by Scott Cunningham and David Harrington

Whether your home is a small apartment or a palatial mansion, you want it to be something special. Now it can be with *The Magical Household*. Learn how to make your home more than just a place to live. Turn it into a place of life and fun and magic. Here you will not find the complex magic of the ceremonial magician. Rather, you will learn simple magical spells that use nothing more than items in your house: furniture, windows, doors, carpet, pets, etc. You will learn to take advantage of the *intrinsic* power and energy that is already in your home, waiting to be tapped. You will learn to make magic a part of your life. The result is a home that is safeguarded from harm and a place which will bring you happiness, health and more.

0-87542-124-5, illustrated, softcover $8.95

THE WISDOM OF SOLOMON THE KING
As interpreted by Priscilla Schwei

Now you can learn to use the deepest secrets of Solomon the King in this kit. It includes a 72-card deck and 200-page book. Together the deck and book allow you to work with the famous 72 *Spirits of Solomon*. The cards each have the name and seal of one of the spirits, as well as astrological, timing, and other information. The book includes cear, easy-to-understand instructions for doing several types of magic, including candle magic, divination, ceremonial magic and the use of talismans. Learn to make use of this powerful system of divination and magic easily and safely.

0-87542-701-4, 200 pgs., 72-card deck   **$14.95**

THE AZTEC CIRCLE OF DESTINY
Bruce Scofield & Angela Cordova

The ancient Mesoamerican calendar and divination system known as the *Tonalpouhalli* has been revived for the third Llewellyn New Worlds Kit by authors Bruce Scofield and Angela Cordova, using both historical research and a fascinating variety of psychic techniques.

⁰The 260-day calendar of the Aztec and Maya civilizations had been buried for centuries through neglect and repression by conquistadores and missionaries. Dream programming, automatic writing, trance work and dowsing all played an important role in the author's reconstruction of associations for each of the twenty day names. The result is a diverse yet complete collection of astrological associations that offers contemporary readers a detailed and entertaining system of divination.

The beautiful images created by Bruce Scofield for the 20-card set are done in the bold colors of ancient Mesoamerican art. Images of the gods adorn the book's pages, which also contain sample card layouts, readings and a complete list of associations for the calendar days. Also included are 13 wooden number chips, a cloth bag and the 20 four-color cards.

0-87542-715-4, 256 pg. book, 13 wooden number chips, 20 cards, cloth bag   **$24.95**

MAGICAL RITES FROM THE CRYSTAL WELL
by Ed Fitch

In nature, and in the Earth, we look and find beauty. Within ourselves we find a well from which we may draw truth and knowledge. And when we draw from this well, we rediscover that we are all children of the Earth.

The simple rites in this book are presented to you as a means of finding your own way back to nature; for discovering and experiencing the beauty and the magic of unity with the source.

These are the celebrations of the seasons: at the same time they are rites by which we attune ourselves to the flow of the force—the energy of life. These are rites of passage by which we celebrate the major transitions we all experience in life.

Here are the Old Ways, but they are also the Ways for Today.

0-87542-230-6, 147 pgs, 7 x 10, illus., softcover. $9.95

PRACTICAL CANDLEBURNING RITUALS
by Raymond Buckland, Ph. D.

Magick is a way in which to apply the full range of your hidden psychic powers to the problems we all face in daily life. We know that normally we use only 5% of our total powers— Magick taps powers from deep inside our psyche where we are in contact with the Universe's limitless resources.

Magick need not be complex—it can be as simple as using a few candles to focus your mind, a simple ritual to give direction to your desire, a few words to give expression to your wish. This book shows you how easy it can be. Here is Magick for fun, Magick as a Craft, Magick for Success, Love, Luck, Money, Marriage, Healing; Magick to stop slander, to learn truth, to heal an unhappy marriage, to overcome a bad habit, to break up a love affair, etc.

Magick—with nothing fancier than ordinary candles, and the 28 rituals in this book (given in both Christian and Old Religion versions)—can transform your life. Illustrated.

0-87542-048-06, 200 pgs., 5¼ x 8, softcover $6.95

STAY IN TOUCH

On the following pages you will find listed, with their current prices, some of the books now available on related subjects. Your book dealer stocks most of these, and will stock new titles in the Llewellyn series as they become available. We urge your patronage.

To obtain a FREE COPY of our latest full CATALOG of New Age books, tapes, videos, products and services, just write to the address below. In each 80-page catalog sent out bimonthly, you will find articles, reviews, the latest information on New Age topics, a listing of news and events, and much more. It is an exciting and informative way to stay in touch with the New Age and the world. The first copy will be sent free of charge and you will continue receiving copies as long as you are an active customer. You may also subscribe to *The Llewellyn New Times* by sending a $5.00 donation ($20.00 for overseas). Order your copy of *The Llewellyn New Times* today!

The Llewellyn New Times
P.O. Box 64383-Dept. 288, St. Paul, MN 55164

TO ORDER BOOKS AND PRODUCTS ON THE FOLLOWING PAGES:

If your book dealer does not carry the titles listed on the following pages, you may order them directly from Llewellyn. Please send full price in U.S. funds, plus $1.50 for postage and handling for orders *under* $10.00; $3.00 for orders *over* $10.00. There are no postage and handling charges for orders over $50. UPS Delivery: We ship UPS whenever possible. Delivery guaranteed. Provide your street address as UPS does not deliver to P.O. Boxes; UPS to Canada requires a $50 minimum order. Allow 4-6 weeks for delivery. Orders outside the USA and Canada: Airmail—add retail price of book; add $5 for each non-book item (tapes, etc.); add $1 per item for surface mail. You may use your major credit card to order these titles by calling 1-800-THE-MOON, M-F, 8:00-5:00, Central Time. Send orders to:

LLEWELLYN PUBLICATIONS
P.O. BOX 64383-288
St. Paul, MN 55164-0383, U.S.A.